Legal Loopholes in India

VOLUME-1

Lawyer Amit Sshuhla

lawyeramitsshukla.com

BLUEROSE PUBLISHERS
U.K.

Copyright © Lawyer Amit Sshukla 2024

All rights reserved by author. No part of this publication may be reproduced, stored in a retrieval system or transmitted in any form or by any means, electronic, mechanical, photocopying, recording or otherwise, without the prior permission of the author. Although every precaution has been taken to verify the accuracy of the information contained herein, the publisher assumes no responsibility for any errors or omissions. No liability is assumed for damages that may result from the use of information contained within.

BlueRose Publishers takes no responsibility for any damages, losses, or liabilities that may arise from the use or misuse of the information, products, or services provided in this publication.

For permissions requests or inquiries regarding this publication, please contact:

BLUEROSE PUBLISHERS
www.BlueRoseONE.com
info@bluerosepublishers.com
+4407342408967

ISBN: 978-93-6783-813-6

Cover design: Daksh
Typesetting: Tanya Raj Upadhyay

First Edition: October 2024

Book Description

"Legal Loopholes in India: Unveiling the Complexities of the Indian Legal System" is a comprehensive and insightful book that delves into the intricacies of the Indian legal system. Written by an expert in Indian laws, this book aims to demystify the complex web of legal loopholes that exist in the country. The book begins by providing a brief overview of the Indian legal system, including its historical development and the various branches of law. It then delves into the concept of legal loopholes, explaining how they arise and the impact they can have on the administration of justice. Through a series of well-researched case studies and real-life examples, the author explores the different types of legal loopholes that exist in India. These include loopholes in criminal law, civil law, corporate law, and constitutional law, among others. The book also examines the role of corruption and political influence in perpetuating these loopholes. Furthermore, "Legal Loopholes in India" offers practical insights and strategies for individuals and businesses to navigate the legal system effectively. It provides guidance on how to identify and exploit legal loopholes ethically, while also highlighting the potential risks and consequences. Written in a clear and accessible language, this book is suitable for both legal professionals and general readers who are interested in understanding the complexities of the Indian legal system. It serves as a valuable resource for anyone seeking to gain a deeper insight into the loopholes that exist within the Indian legal framework and how they can be addressed.

The author meticulously examines the gaps and inconsistencies in the law, which often lead to confusion and exploitation. Through real-life case studies and examples, the book illustrates how these loopholes can be exploited by individuals and corporations to their advantage. Furthermore, the book also addresses the challenges faced by individuals seeking justice within the Indian legal system. It discusses the lengthy and cumbersome legal procedures, the backlog of cases, and the lack of access to justice for marginalized sections of society. The author offers practical advice and strategies for individuals to navigate these challenges effectively. In addition to analyzing the loopholes, the book also provides insights into recent legal reforms and landmark judgments that have shaped the Indian legal system. It explores the impact of these reforms on various sectors, such as business, human rights, and social justice.

Table of Contents

Introduction 1

Chapter 1. Understanding the Indian Legal System. ... 3
   1.1 Historical Overview of Indian Laws 4
   1.2 Structure of the Indian Legal System 6
   1.3 Role of the Judiciary 7
   1.4 Legislative Process in India 9
   1.5 Executive and Administrative Laws 10

Chapter 2: Exploring Legal Loopholes 13
   2.1 Definition and Types of Legal Loopholes 13
   2.2 Factors Contributing to Legal Loopholes in India . 15
   2.3 Impact of Legal Loopholes on Justice and Society 16
   2.4 Case Studies: Notorious Legal Loopholes in India 18

Chapter 3: Criminal Law Loopholes 21
   3.1 Bail and Pre-trial Release 22
   3.2 Plea Bargaining and Leniency 23
   3.3 Inadequate Investigation and Evidence Collection. 25
   3.4 Sentencing Disparities 26
   3.5 Corruption and Influence on Legal Proceedings 28

Chapter 4: Civil Law Loopholes 31
   4.1 Contractual Ambiguities and Interpretation 32
   4.2 Delay Tactics and Procedural Loopholes 33

4.3 Ineffective Enforcement of Judgments 35
4.4 Arbitration and Mediation Loopholes 36
4.5 Fraud and Misrepresentation in Civil Cases 38

Chapter 5: Constitutional Law Loopholes 40
5.1 Fundamental Rights and their Limitations 41
5.2 Judicial Activism and Interpretation 43
5.3 Legislative Overreach and Constitutional Amendments 44
5.4 Reservation Policies and Affirmative Action 45
5.5 Freedom of Speech and Expression 47

Chapter 6: Administrative Law Loopholes 49
6.1 Administrative Discretion and Abuse of Power 50
6.2 Lack of Transparency and Accountability 52
6.3 Red Tape and Bureaucratic Delays 53
6.4 Public Interest Litigation and its Misuse 55
6.5 Environmental Regulations and Compliance 56

Chapter 7: Intellectual Property Law Loopholes 59
7.1 Patent and Copyright Infringement 60
7.2 Trademark and Trade Secret Violations 61
7.3 Piracy and Counterfeiting 63
7.4 Challenges in Enforcement and Protection 64
7.5 International Intellectual Property Law Discrepancies 66

Chapter 8: Taxation Law Loopholes 69
   8.1 Tax Evasion and Avoidance Strategies 70

   8.2 Transfer Pricing and Shell Companies 72

   8.3 Black Money and Offshore Accounts 73

   8.4 Double Taxation Agreements 74

   8.5 Taxation of Digital Economy 76

Chapter 9: Land and Property Law Loopholes 78
   9.1 Land Acquisition and Rehabilitation 79

   9.2 Encroachment and Illegal Constructions 81

   9.3 Title Disputes and Fraudulent Transfers............... 82

   9.4 Rent Control and Tenancy Laws 83

   9.5 Real Estate Regulation and Development............. 85

Chapter 10: Reforms and Solutions 87
   10.1 Judicial Reforms and Case Management 89

   10.2 Legislative Amendments and Policy Changes..... 91

   10.3 Strengthening Law Enforcement and Investigation... 92

   10.4 Public Awareness and Legal Education.............. 94

   10.5 International Cooperation and Comparative Studies... 96

Introduction

The Indian legal system is known for its complexity and intricacies, which often gives rise to legal loopholes. These loopholes refer to the gaps or inconsistencies in the law that allow individuals or entities to exploit or circumvent legal requirements or obligations. They can be unintentional or deliberate, and pose significant challenges to the effective implementation and enforcement of laws in India.

One of the main reasons for the existence of legal loopholes in India is the vast and diverse nature of the country. India is a federal republic with 28 states and 8 union territories, each having its own set of laws and regulations. This decentralized legal framework often leads to inconsistencies and contradictions between different laws, creating opportunities for individuals to exploit these gaps. Another factor contributing to legal loopholes is the slow and cumbersome legal process in India. The Indian legal system is notorious for its backlog of cases and delays in delivering justice. This delay provides individuals with ample time to manipulate the system and find ways to exploit the legal loopholes to their advantage.

Furthermore, the lack of clarity and specificity in some laws also contributes to the existence of legal loopholes. Vague or ambiguous language in legislation can be interpreted in different ways, allowing individuals to exploit these loopholes by finding alternative interpretations that favor their interests. Additionally, corruption and bribery play a significant role in the creation and exploitation of legal loopholes in India. Unscrupulous individuals often bribe officials or manipulate the legal process to their advantage, thereby evading legal obligations or securing favorable outcomes.

Legal loopholes can be found in various areas of Indian law, including taxation, property rights, criminal law, and corporate regulations. For example, in the realm of taxation, individuals may exploit loopholes to evade taxes by taking advantage of ambiguous provisions or using complex financial structures. The existence of legal loopholes poses significant challenges to the Indian legal system. It undermines the rule of law, erodes public trust, and hampers the effective implementation of legislation. Addressing these loopholes requires comprehensive legal reforms, including the simplification and harmonization of laws, strengthening of enforcement mechanisms, and promoting transparency and accountability in the legal system. In conclusion, legal loopholes in India are a result of the complex and decentralized nature of the legal system, delays in the legal process, vague legislation, and corruption.

These loopholes undermine the effectiveness of laws and pose challenges to the implementation of justice. Addressing these loopholes requires systemic reforms to ensure a more transparent, efficient, and accountable legal system in India.

Chapter 1.
Understanding the Indian Legal System.

The Indian legal system is a complex framework that governs the laws and regulations in India. It is based on a combination of common law, which is derived from British legal principles, and various codified laws. The Constitution of India is the supreme law of the land and provides the framework for the legal system. It establishes the structure and powers of the government, as well as the fundamental rights and duties of citizens. The Constitution also sets out the division of powers between the central government and the state governments.

The Indian legal system is divided into three main branches: the judiciary, the legislature, and the executive.

The judiciary is independent and is responsible for interpreting and applying the laws. It consists of the Supreme Court, which is the highest court in the country, and various high courts at the state level. The judiciary also includes subordinate courts, such as district courts and lower courts, which handle civil and criminal cases.

The legislature is responsible for making laws. It consists of the Parliament at the central level and the state legislatures at the state level. The Parliament is divided into two houses: the Lok Sabha (House of the People) and the Rajya Sabha (Council of States). The Parliament has the power to enact laws on various subjects, including criminal law, civil law, and constitutional matters.

The executive branch is responsible for implementing and enforcing the laws. It consists of the President, who is the head of state, and the Prime Minister, who is the head of government. The executive branch also includes various ministries and departments that are responsible for specific areas of governance. In addition to the Constitution, India has a comprehensive legal framework that includes various laws and regulations. These laws cover a wide range of subjects, including criminal law, civil law, family law, property law, contract law, labor law, and taxation law.

The Indian legal system also incorporates principles of equity and natural justice. It provides for the protection of fundamental rights, such as the right to equality, freedom of speech, and the right to life and personal liberty. It also includes provisions for the resolution of disputes through alternative methods, such as mediation and arbitration. Overall, the Indian legal system is a complex and evolving framework that plays a crucial role in maintaining law and order, protecting individual rights, and promoting justice in the country.

1.1 Historical Overview of Indian Laws

The history of Indian laws can be traced back to the ancient times, with the development of legal systems influenced by various rulers and civilizations that have ruled the Indian subcontinent. Here is a brief historical overview of Indian laws:

Ancient Period (2500 BCE - 600 CE): During this period, ancient Indian society was governed by an intricate legal system known as Dharma. Dharma encompassed religious, moral, and legal principles and was based on texts such as the Vedas, Manusmriti, and Arthashastra. The legal system focused on maintaining social order and justice.

Medieval Period (600 CE - 1700 CE): With the advent of Islamic rule in India, Islamic law, known as Sharia, began to influence the legal system. Islamic rulers introduced their own legal codes, which coexisted with the existing Hindu legal systems. The legal system during this period was a blend of Hindu and Islamic laws.

Colonial Period (1700 CE - 1947 CE): The British East India Company established its presence in India in the 17th century and gradually gained control over large parts of the country. The British introduced their own legal system, based on English common law, to administer justice. The British enacted various laws, such as the Indian Penal Code (IPC) in 1860 and the Code of Criminal Procedure (CrPC) in 1861, which continued to be the foundation of the Indian legal system.

Post-Independence Period (1947 CE - Present): India gained independence from British rule in 1947 and adopted a new constitution in 1950. The Indian Constitution became the supreme law of the land and provided for a democratic and secular state. The constitution established a federal system with a division of powers between the central government and the states. It also guaranteed fundamental rights to its citizens and established an independent judiciary. Since independence, the Indian legal system has undergone significant reforms and developments. New laws have been enacted to address various social, economic, and political issues. The judiciary plays a crucial role in interpreting and upholding the constitution and ensuring the rule of law. Today, Indian laws cover a wide range of areas, including but not limited to criminal law, civil law, family law, property law, labor law, environmental law, and intellectual property law. The legal system is a mix of statutory laws, case laws, and customary laws, with the Supreme Court of India being the highest judicial authority in the country.

1.2 Structure of the Indian Legal System

The Indian legal system is a hierarchical structure that is based on a combination of written laws, precedents, and customs. It is primarily derived from the British legal system, but also incorporates elements of Hindu, Muslim, and other indigenous laws.

The structure of the Indian legal system can be broadly divided into three main components:

1. Supreme Court of India: At the top of the hierarchy is the Supreme Court of India, which is the highest judicial authority in the country. It has the power of judicial review and is responsible for interpreting the Constitution and ensuring its enforcement. The Supreme Court consists of a Chief Justice and a maximum of 34 judges.

2. High Courts: Each state in India has its own High Court, which is the highest judicial authority within the state. High Courts have the power of superintendence over all subordinate courts and tribunals within their jurisdiction.

They also have the power to issue writs for the enforcement of fundamental rights.

3. Subordinate Courts: Below the High Courts are the subordinate courts, which include District Courts, Sessions Courts, and other specialized courts and tribunals. These courts are responsible for the administration of justice at the district and local levels. They handle both civil and criminal cases and are presided over by judges recommended by the High Courts.

In addition to these three main components, there are also various specialized courts and tribunals in India, such as the National Green Tribunal, the National Company Law Tribunal, and the Consumer Disputes Redressal Forums. These specialized courts have jurisdiction over specific areas of law and provide speedy and efficient resolution of disputes. The Indian legal system is governed by a combination of statutory laws, which are enacted by the Parliament and state legislatures, and case laws, which are derived from judicial decisions. The Constitution of India is the supreme law of the land and provides the framework for the legal system. It guarantees fundamental rights to all citizens and establishes the powers and functions of the various branches of government. Overall, the structure of the Indian legal system is designed to ensure the rule of law, protect individual rights, and provide access to justice for all citizens.

1.3 Role of the Judiciary

The judiciary plays a crucial role in the Indian legal system. Its primary role is to interpret and apply the laws of the country, ensuring justice and upholding the rule of law. The judiciary provides check and balance on the other branches of government, namely the executive and legislative branches. Some of the key roles and functions of the judiciary in India include:

1. Interpreting the Constitution: The judiciary has the power to interpret the provisions of the Constitution and determine their applicability in various cases. This helps in safeguarding the fundamental rights and principles enshrined in the Constitution.

2. Adjudicating disputes: The judiciary resolves disputes between individuals, organizations, and the state. It ensures that justice is served by impartially hearing both sides of the argument and making fair and unbiased decisions.

3. Judicial review: The judiciary has the power of judicial review, which allows it to review the constitutionality of laws and executive actions. It ensures that the laws and actions of the government are in line with the Constitution and do not violate the rights of individuals.

4. Protecting fundamental rights: The judiciary acts as the guardian of fundamental rights guaranteed by the Constitution. It protects the rights of citizens and ensures that they are not violated by the state or any other entity.

5. Upholding the rule of law: The judiciary ensures that the rule of law is upheld in the country. It ensures that laws are applied uniformly and that no one is above the law, including the government and its officials.

6. Setting legal precedents: The judiciary's decisions in various cases set legal precedents, which serve as guidelines for future cases. These precedents help in

maintaining consistency and predictability in the legal system.

7. Judicial activism: In certain cases, the judiciary may take an active role in addressing social and public interest issues.

This is known as judicial activism, where the judiciary goes beyond its traditional role and actively participates in shaping public policy. Overall, the judiciary in India plays a vital role in ensuring justice, protecting rights, and upholding the rule of law. It acts as a safeguard against any abuse of power by the government and ensures that the legal system functions effectively and fairly.

1.4 Legislative Process in India

The legislative process in India involves the creation and enactment of laws by the Parliament of India. The Parliament consists of two houses: the Lok Sabha (House of the People) and the Rajya Sabha (Council of States).

The legislative process begins with the introduction of a bill in either house of Parliament. A bill is a proposal for a new law or an amendment to an existing law. Bills can be introduced by ministers or private members. Once a bill is introduced, it goes through several stages before it becomes a law.

The first stage is the introduction stage, where the bill is presented to the house and its objectives and reasons are explained. After the bill is introduced, it goes through the second stage, known as the committee stage. In this stage, the bill is examined in detail by a committee of members from the house. The committee may suggest amendments or modifications to the bill. After the committee stage, the bill goes through the third stage, which is the report stage. In this stage, the committee presents its report on the bill to the house. The members of the house then have an opportunity to discuss and debate the bill, and propose further amendments if necessary. The fourth stage is the consideration stage, where the bill is further debated and amendments are made. After the consideration stage, the bill goes through the fifth stage, which is the voting stage. Members of the house vote on the bill, and if it is passed by a majority, it moves to the other house for consideration.

The bill goes through a similar process in the other house, including the introduction, committee, report, consideration, and voting stages. If both houses pass the bill with the same text, it is sent to the President of India for assent. Once the President gives assent, the bill becomes an act of Parliament and is enforceable as law. However, if the President withholds assent, the bill can be sent back to Parliament for reconsideration. If both houses pass the bill again with or without amendments, the President is bound to give assent. Overall, the legislative process in India is a multi-stage process that involves the introduction, committee examination, debate, and voting on bills in both houses of Parliament before they become a law.

1.5 Executive and Administrative Laws

Executive and administrative laws in India refer to the laws and regulations that are formulated and implemented by the executive branch of the government. These laws are primarily concerned with the day-to-day functioning of the government and the administration of various government departments and agencies. The executive branch of the government in India consists of the President, the Prime Minister, the Council of Ministers, and the various ministries and departments under them.

The executive branch is responsible for implementing and enforcing laws passed by the legislature, as well as formulating and implementing policies and regulations to govern various aspects of governance and administration. Executive and administrative laws cover a wide range of areas, including but not limited to:

1. Administrative procedures: These laws govern the procedures and processes followed by government departments and agencies in carrying out their functions. They include rules and regulations related to recruitment, promotion, transfer, and discipline of government employees, as well as procedures for decision-making, public procurement, and contract management.

2. Public finance and budgeting: These laws regulate the management of public funds, including budget preparation, expenditure control, accounting, and auditing. They also cover taxation and revenue collection, as well as financial management in government departments and agencies.

3. Public service delivery: These laws govern the provision of public services by government departments and agencies, including healthcare, education, transportation, and public utilities. They establish standards and regulations for service delivery, as well as mechanisms for monitoring and evaluation.

4. Regulatory frameworks: These laws establish regulatory bodies and frameworks to oversee and regulate various sectors of the economy, such as telecommunications,

banking, insurance, securities, and environmental protection. They define the powers and functions of regulatory authorities and set out rules and regulations for the operation of regulated entities.

5. Public safety and security: These laws cover areas such as law enforcement, national security, disaster management, and emergency response. They establish the powers and responsibilities of law enforcement agencies, as well as procedures for maintaining public order and ensuring public safety.

Executive and administrative laws are essential for the effective functioning of the government and the delivery of public services. They provide the legal framework within which government departments and agencies operate and ensure accountability, transparency, and efficiency in governance and administration.

Chapter 2:
Exploring Legal Loopholes

Exploring legal loopholes refers to the act of searching for and exploiting gaps or inconsistencies in the law to gain an advantage or avoid legal consequences. It involves finding ways to circumvent or manipulate the law's intended purpose or requirements. However, it is important to note that actively seeking and exploiting legal loopholes can be unethical and may lead to legal consequences. Laws are designed to maintain order, protect individuals' rights, and promote justice. Exploiting loopholes can undermine these principles and harm society as a whole. In India, as in any other country, the legal system is constantly evolving to address new challenges and close existing loopholes. The judiciary and legislative bodies work together to interpret and amend laws to ensure their effectiveness and fairness. It is advisable to consult with legal professionals and abide by the spirit and intent of the law rather than attempting to exploit loopholes.

2.1 Definition and Types of Legal Loopholes

A legal loophole refers to a technicality or ambiguity in the law that allows individuals or entities to exploit or circumvent the intended purpose or effect of a law. It is a gap or inconsistency in the legal system that can be used to gain an advantage or avoid legal consequences.

There are various types of legal loopholes, including:

1. Ambiguity: When a law is poorly drafted or contains vague language, it can create loopholes that can be interpreted in different ways. This ambiguity allows individuals to exploit the law's weaknesses and find alternative interpretations that favor their interests.

2. Legislative Oversight: Sometimes, lawmakers may unintentionally overlook certain scenarios or fail to address specific situations in the law. This oversight can create loopholes that individuals can exploit to their advantage.

3. Technicalities: Legal loopholes can also arise from technicalities or procedural errors. For example, a defendant may be acquitted due to a technicality in the evidence or a failure to follow proper legal procedures.

4. Jurisdictional Differences: Different jurisdictions may have different laws or legal systems. Individuals can exploit these jurisdictional differences by engaging in activities that are legal in one jurisdiction but illegal in another.

5. Tax Loopholes: Tax laws often contain loopholes that allow individuals or businesses to minimize their tax liability. These loopholes can be exploited through various means, such as using offshore accounts or taking advantage of tax deductions and exemptions.

6. Regulatory Gaps: Sometimes, laws and regulations fail to keep up with technological advancements or changing societal norms. These regulatory gaps can create loopholes that individuals can exploit to engage in activities that are not explicitly prohibited by the law. It is important to note that while legal loopholes may provide individuals with opportunities to avoid legal consequences, they are not always considered ethical or morally acceptable.

Governments and legal authorities often strive to identify and close loopholes to ensure the fair and effective implementation of the law.

2.2 Factors Contributing to Legal Loopholes in India

There are several factors contributing to legal loopholes in India. Some of the key factors include:

1. Complexity of laws: Indian laws are often complex and convoluted, making it difficult for individuals to understand and comply with them. This complexity creates loopholes that can be exploited by those with legal knowledge and resources.

2. Outdated laws: Many Indian laws are outdated and have not kept pace with the changing social, economic, and technological landscape. This creates gaps and inconsistencies that can be exploited by individuals or entities to circumvent the law.

3. Lack of enforcement: Even when laws exist to address certain issues, the lack of effective enforcement mechanisms often leads to loopholes. Weak enforcement allows individuals or entities to engage in illegal activities without fear of consequences.

4. Corruption: Corruption is a significant factor contributing to legal loopholes in India. Bribery and other forms of corruption can influence the legal system, leading to compromised enforcement and the creation of loopholes for those who can afford to pay.

5. Overburdened judiciary: The Indian judiciary is burdened with a large number of pending cases, leading to delays in the resolution of legal disputes. This backlog creates opportunities for individuals to exploit legal loopholes and prolong legal proceedings.

6. Lack of legal awareness: Many people in India are not aware of their legal rights and obligations. This lack of awareness makes them vulnerable to exploitation and manipulation, leading to the creation of legal loopholes.

7. Political influence: Political influence can also contribute to legal loopholes in India. Politically connected individuals or entities may be able to influence the creation or amendment of laws to suit their interests, creating loopholes that benefit them.

8. Lack of coordination between different legal frameworks: India has multiple legal frameworks, including central and state laws, as well as different laws for different sectors. The lack of coordination and harmonization between these frameworks can create gaps and inconsistencies that can be exploited. Addressing these factors requires comprehensive legal reforms, including simplification and modernization of laws, strengthening of enforcement mechanisms, tackling corruption, improving legal awareness, and ensuring effective coordination between different legal frameworks.

2.3 Impact of Legal Loopholes on Justice and Society

Legal loopholes refer to gaps or inconsistencies in the law that allow individuals or entities to exploit or circumvent the intended purpose or spirit of the law. These loopholes can have a significant impact on justice and society in several ways:

1. Inequality and Injustice: Legal loopholes can lead to unequal treatment under the law. Those who are aware of and can afford to exploit these loopholes may receive preferential treatment or escape punishment, while others who are unaware or unable to exploit them may face harsh consequences. This undermines the principle of equality before the law and erodes public trust in the justice system.

2. Impunity and Corruption: Loopholes can create opportunities for corruption and abuse of power. Individuals in positions of authority may exploit these gaps to engage in illegal activities without fear of prosecution. This can lead to a culture of impunity, where the powerful can act with impunity, undermining the rule of law and fostering a sense of injustice in society.

3. Delayed Justice: Loopholes can also contribute to delays in the justice system. Legal battles may be prolonged as parties exploit these gaps to their advantage, leading to a backlog of cases and a slow dispensation of justice. This can result in frustration and disillusionment among the public, as justice is not served in a timely manner.

4. Erosion of Public Confidence: Legal loopholes can erode public confidence in the justice system. When people perceive that the law is not being applied fairly or that certain individuals or groups are able to manipulate the system, it undermines trust in the legal system. This can lead to a breakdown in social cohesion and a loss of faith in

the ability of the law to protect and serve the interests of society.

5. Inefficiency and Ineffectiveness: Loopholes can render laws and regulations ineffective in achieving their intended goals. When individuals or entities can easily evade the law, it hampers the ability of the legal system to address social problems and protect the rights of individuals. This can result in a lack of deterrence and a perpetuation of harmful practices or behaviors.

To address the impact of legal loopholes on justice and society, it is crucial to regularly review and update laws to close any gaps or inconsistencies. Additionally, strengthening enforcement mechanisms, promoting transparency, and enhancing public awareness and education about legal rights and responsibilities can help mitigate the negative effects of loopholes.

2.4 Case Studies: Notorious Legal Loopholes in India

1. The Dowry Prohibition Act: The Dowry Prohibition Act was enacted in 1961 to prohibit the giving or taking of dowry in marriages. However, there have been numerous cases where individuals have found loopholes in the law to continue the practice. For example, instead of giving dowry in cash or assets, families may give expensive gifts or provide financial support in other forms, which technically do not fall under the definition of dowry.

2. Section 498A of the Indian Penal Code: Section 498A deals with cruelty against married women by their husbands or in-laws. While the intention of the law is to protect

women from domestic violence, there have been instances where it has been misused. False allegations of cruelty have been made by some women to settle personal scores or gain an advantage in divorce or custody battles. This has led to innocent individuals being falsely accused and facing legal consequences.

3. Section 377 of the Indian Penal Code: Section 377 criminalized consensual homosexual acts between adults until it was decriminalized by the Supreme Court in 2018. However, the law still leaves room for ambiguity and potential misuse. For instance, individuals can still be charged under this section for non-consensual acts or for engaging in public displays of affection, which can be subjective and open to interpretation.

4. The Juvenile Justice Act: The Juvenile Justice Act was enacted to protect the rights of children and ensure their rehabilitation and reintegration into society. However, there have been cases where juveniles involved in heinous crimes have taken advantage of the leniency provided by the law. The act sets a maximum punishment of three years for juveniles, regardless of the severity of the crime committed, which has led to debates on whether the law adequately addresses the issue of juvenile crime.

5. The Right to Information Act: The Right to Information (RTI) Act was introduced to promote transparency and accountability in government institutions. However, there have been instances where public authorities have used loopholes in the law to deny or delay access to information. Some authorities have also misused exemptions provided under the act to withhold information that should be in the public domain, undermining the purpose of the legislation.

It is important to note that while these loopholes exist, efforts are continuously being made to address them and improve the legal system in India.

Chapter 3:
Criminal Law Loopholes

Criminal law loopholes refer to legal gaps or ambiguities that can be exploited by individuals accused of committing a crime to avoid conviction or receive a lesser punishment. These loopholes can arise due to various reasons, such as inadequate legislation, procedural errors, or inconsistencies in the law. It is important to note that the exploitation of loopholes does not necessarily imply innocence or exoneration of the accused; rather, it highlights flaws in the legal system that can be manipulated. In the context of Indian laws, some common criminal law loopholes include:

1. Lack of evidence: If the prosecution fails to present sufficient evidence to prove the guilt of the accused beyond reasonable doubt, it can create a loophole for the defense to argue for acquittal.

2. Procedural errors: Any mistakes or violations of procedural rules during the investigation, arrest, or trial can lead to the exclusion of evidence or dismissal of the case.

3. Violation of constitutional rights: If the accused's constitutional rights, such as the right to a fair trial, right against self-incrimination, or right to legal representation, are violated, it can provide grounds for challenging the legality of the proceedings.

4. Insanity defense: In cases where the accused can establish that they were mentally incapable of

understanding the nature and consequences of their actions at the time of the offense, they may be able to use the insanity defense to avoid criminal liability.

5. Plea bargaining: The option of plea bargaining allows the accused to negotiate a plea deal with the prosecution, often resulting in a reduced charge or sentence in exchange for a guilty plea. This can be seen as a loophole as it allows the accused to avoid a potentially harsher punishment.

It is important to note that the legal system continually evolves to address and close these loopholes. Courts and lawmakers work towards ensuring that the law is comprehensive, fair, and effective in delivering justice.

3.1 Bail and Pre-trial Release

Bail and pre-trial release are legal concepts in Indian law that pertain to the release of an accused person from custody before their trial. These concepts are based on the principle that a person is presumed innocent until proven guilty and should not be unnecessarily detained. Bail refers to the temporary release of an accused person from custody, usually upon the deposit of a sum of money or the provision of a guarantee. The purpose of bail is to ensure the presence of the accused at their trial and to prevent them from fleeing or tampering with evidence. Bail can be granted at various stages of the criminal justice process, including during the investigation, after the filing of charges, or during the trial. The granting of bail is at the discretion of the court, and several factors are considered in making this decision. These factors include the seriousness of the offense, the likelihood of the accused fleeing, the potential danger posed by the accused to society, the strength of the evidence against the accused, and the accused's criminal record. Bail can be denied if the court believes that the accused is a flight risk or a danger to society.

Pre-trial release, on the other hand, refers to the release of an accused person from custody without the requirement of bail. This can be granted in cases where the offense is not serious, the accused has strong ties to the community, and there is a low risk of flight or danger to society. Pre-trial release can also be granted with certain conditions, such as regular reporting to the police, surrendering of travel documents, or restrictions on contact with witnesses.

It is important to note that bail and pre-trial release are not absolute rights, and the court has the authority to deny or revoke these privileges if there is a change in circumstances or if the accused violates the conditions of their release. Additionally, bail can be forfeited if the accused fails to appear in court as required. The specific provisions and procedures regarding bail and pre-trial release are outlined in the Code of Criminal Procedure, 1973, and are subject to interpretation by the courts.

3.2 Plea Bargaining and Leniency

Plea bargaining and leniency are two concepts within the Indian legal system that aim to expedite the judicial process and provide certain benefits to accused individuals.

Plea Bargaining: Plea bargaining is a negotiation process between the prosecution and the accused, where the accused agrees to plead guilty in exchange for certain concessions from the prosecution. This process allows for a quicker resolution of cases and reduces the burden on the courts. Plea bargaining is governed by the Code of Criminal Procedure (CrPC) in India. Under the Indian legal system, plea bargaining is available for certain offenses that are punishable with imprisonment for a term of seven years or less. The accused can approach the court expressing their willingness to plead guilty, and the court may then refer the case to the plea bargaining committee for further negotiations. If an agreement is reached, the court may pass a sentence based on the terms of the plea bargain.

Leniency: Leniency refers to the concept of granting a more lenient punishment or sentence to an accused individual. This can be done based on various factors, such as the accused's cooperation with the investigation, remorse, or other mitigating circumstances. Leniency is typically considered during the sentencing stage of a criminal trial. In India, the principle of leniency is recognized under the Indian Penal Code (IPC) and the Code of Criminal Procedure (CrPC). The court has the discretion to consider factors such as the nature of the offense, the accused's background, and any other relevant circumstances while determining the appropriate punishment. The court may choose to impose a lesser sentence or consider alternative forms of punishment, such as probation or community service, based on the principle of leniency.

It is important to note that plea bargaining and leniency are separate concepts, although they can sometimes be interconnected. Plea bargaining primarily focuses on resolving cases through negotiation, while leniency pertains to the sentencing stage and the discretion of the court in determining the punishment.

3.3 Inadequate Investigation and Evidence Collection

Inadequate investigation and evidence collection refer to the failure of law enforcement agencies or authorities to conduct a thorough and comprehensive investigation into a crime or incident, resulting in a lack of sufficient evidence to support a conviction or establish guilt beyond a reasonable doubt. In India, the Code of Criminal Procedure (CrPC) governs the investigation process, and the Indian Evidence Act regulates the collection and admissibility of evidence in criminal cases. However, despite these legal provisions, there have been instances where investigations have been deemed inadequate, leading to miscarriages of justice.

There are several reasons why investigations may be inadequate in India. These include:

1. Lack of resources: Law enforcement agencies often face resource constraints, such as a shortage of personnel, outdated equipment, and limited forensic capabilities. These limitations can hinder the collection and analysis of evidence, leading to incomplete investigations.

2. Corruption and misconduct: Instances of corruption and misconduct within law enforcement agencies can compromise the integrity of investigations. This can include tampering with evidence, fabricating witness statements, or protecting influential individuals involved in the crime.

3. Incompetence and lack of training: In some cases, investigators may lack the necessary skills, knowledge, or training to conduct a thorough investigation. This can result

in crucial evidence being overlooked or mishandled, leading to a weak case.

4. Pressure to close cases quickly: There is often pressure on law enforcement agencies to solve cases quickly, particularly high-profile or politically sensitive ones. This can lead to shortcuts being taken during the investigation process, compromising the quality and reliability of the evidence collected.

The consequences of inadequate investigation and evidence collection can be severe. Innocent individuals may be wrongfully convicted, while guilty parties may go unpunished. This not only undermines the credibility of the criminal justice system but also denies justice to the victims and their families. Efforts have been made to address these issues in recent years.

The Supreme Court of India has emphasized the importance of fair and thorough investigations, and various guidelines and directives have been issued to ensure the proper collection and preservation of evidence. Additionally, the use of technology, such as forensic tools and digital evidence analysis, is being increasingly employed to strengthen investigations. However, despite these measures, challenges remain, and there is a need for continuous improvement in the investigation and evidence collection processes to ensure a fair and effective criminal justice system in India.

3.4 Sentencing Disparities

Sentencing disparities refer to the differences in the penalties imposed on individuals convicted of similar crimes. These disparities can arise due to various factors, including race, gender, socioeconomic status, and geographic location. In India, sentencing disparities have been a matter of concern and debate. There have been instances where individuals from marginalized communities or lower socioeconomic backgrounds have received harsher punishments compared to those from privileged backgrounds for similar offenses. This has raised questions about the fairness and impartiality of the criminal justice system.

One factor contributing to sentencing disparities in India is the discretionary power of judges. The Indian Penal Code provides a wide range of punishments for different offenses, allowing judges to exercise their discretion in determining the appropriate sentence. However, this discretion can sometimes lead to inconsistencies and disparities in sentencing.

Another factor is the lack of uniform sentencing guidelines. Unlike some other countries, India does not have comprehensive guidelines or sentencing grids that provide clear criteria for judges to determine the appropriate punishment. This lack of guidelines can result in subjective decision-making and disparities in sentencing. Additionally, societal biases and prejudices can influence sentencing outcomes. There have been instances where individuals from marginalized communities, such as Dalits or religious minorities, have faced discrimination in the criminal justice system, leading to harsher punishments. Efforts have been made to address sentencing disparities in India.

The Supreme Court has emphasized the need for consistency and proportionality in sentencing and has issued guidelines to ensure fairness. The Law Commission of India has also recommended the establishment of sentencing guidelines to promote uniformity and transparency in sentencing. However, despite these efforts, sentencing disparities continue to be a challenge in the Indian criminal justice system. Addressing these disparities requires ongoing efforts to promote equality, fairness, and transparency in the sentencing process.

3.5 Corruption and Influence on Legal Proceedings

Corruption is a significant issue in many legal systems around the world, including India. It refers to the abuse of power or position for personal gain, often involving bribery, fraud, or other unethical practices. Corruption can have a detrimental impact on legal proceedings, undermining the principles of justice, fairness, and equality before the law.

Influence on Legal Proceedings:

1. Delaying or Manipulating Cases: Corrupt individuals may use their influence to delay or manipulate legal proceedings to their advantage. This can involve bribing judges, lawyers, or other court officials to ensure favorable outcomes or to prolong the process to the detriment of the opposing party.

2. Bias and Unfairness: Corruption can lead to biased decision-making, where judges or other legal authorities are influenced by personal interests or external pressures. This can result in unfair treatment of parties involved in legal proceedings, compromising the integrity of the justice system.

3. Suppression of Evidence: Corrupt individuals may attempt to suppress or manipulate evidence to protect themselves or their associates. This can involve tampering with documents, bribing witnesses, or obstructing the investigation process, leading to miscarriages of justice.

4. Lack of Accountability: Corruption can create a culture of impunity, where those involved in illegal activities are shielded from prosecution or punishment. This lack of accountability erodes public trust in the legal system and undermines the rule of law.

Efforts to Combat Corruption: The Indian legal system recognizes the need to address corruption and has implemented various measures to combat it. These include:

1. Anti-Corruption Laws: India has enacted several laws to tackle corruption, such as the Prevention of Corruption Act, 1988, and the Lokpal and Lokayuktas Act, 2013. These laws aim to prevent, investigate, and punish corrupt practices in both the public and private sectors.

2. Independent Anti-Corruption Bodies: Institutions like the Central Bureau of Investigation (CBI) and the Central Vigilance Commission (CVC) have been established to investigate corruption cases and ensure accountability.

3. Judicial Reforms: The judiciary has taken steps to enhance transparency and accountability within the legal system. This includes the introduction of e-courts, video conferencing for hearings, and the establishment of special anti-corruption courts to expedite corruption cases.

4. Whistleblower Protection: The Whistleblower Protection Act, 2014, provides safeguards for individuals who expose

corruption or wrongdoing. It encourages the reporting of corrupt practices and offers protection to whistleblowers from victimization. Despite these efforts, corruption continues to be a challenge in the Indian legal system. Addressing this issue requires sustained commitment from all stakeholders, including the government, judiciary, law enforcement agencies, and the public.

Chapter 4:
Civil Law Loopholes

Civil law loopholes refer to gaps or weaknesses in the legal system that allow individuals or entities to exploit or circumvent the law for their own benefit. These loopholes can be unintentional or intentional and can be used to evade legal obligations, manipulate legal processes, or gain an unfair advantage in civil disputes.

Some common examples of civil law loopholes include:

1. Ambiguous or vague language in contracts or legal documents: Loopholes can arise when the wording of a contract or legal document is unclear or open to interpretation. This can allow parties to exploit the ambiguity to their advantage or to avoid fulfilling their obligations.

2. Jurisdictional loopholes: Different jurisdictions may have different laws or regulations, and individuals or entities may exploit these differences to their advantage. They may choose to file a lawsuit in a jurisdiction with more favorable laws or regulations, or they may engage in forum shopping to find a court that is more likely to rule in their favor.

3. Timing loopholes: Loopholes can arise due to delays or gaps in the legal process. For example, if a statute of limitations has expired, a party may be able to avoid legal consequences for their actions.

4. Asset protection loopholes: Individuals or entities may use legal structures or strategies to protect their assets from creditors or legal claims. These strategies may involve transferring assets to family members or creating complex corporate structures to shield assets from potential liabilities.

5. Tax loopholes: Tax laws can be complex, and individuals or businesses may exploit loopholes to minimize their tax liabilities. This can involve taking advantage of deductions, exemptions, or offshore tax havens. It is important to note that while loopholes may exist in civil law, they are not necessarily illegal. However, they can be seen as unethical or unfair, and efforts are often made to close these loopholes through legislative reforms or court decisions.

4.1 Contractual Ambiguities and Interpretation

Contractual ambiguities refer to situations where the terms or provisions of a contract are unclear, vague, or open to multiple interpretations. These ambiguities can arise due to various reasons, such as poorly drafted clauses, conflicting provisions, or the use of ambiguous language. When faced with contractual ambiguities, the courts or arbitrators may resort to the principles of contract interpretation to determine the intended meaning of the contract. In India, the interpretation of contracts is governed by the Indian Contract Act, 1872, and the principles of common law.

The primary objective of contract interpretation is to ascertain the intention of the parties at the time of entering into the contract. The courts will consider the language used in the contract, the surrounding circumstances, the purpose of the contract, and the conduct of the parties to determine the true meaning of the contract.

In case of an ambiguity, the courts will adopt an interpretation that gives effect to the intention of the parties and avoids rendering any provision of the contract meaningless or redundant. The courts will also consider the reasonable expectations of the parties and the commercial purpose of the contract. In interpreting a contract, the courts may also consider extrinsic evidence, such as prior negotiations, industry customs, and trade usage, to understand the context and meaning of the contract. However, the courts will not consider evidence that contradicts the express terms of the contract. If the ambiguity cannot be resolved through interpretation, the courts may resort to the doctrine of contra proferentem, which means that any ambiguity in a contract will be construed against the party who drafted the contract or imposed the ambiguous term. It is important for parties to a contract to ensure that the terms are clear, unambiguous, and accurately reflect their intentions. This can be achieved through careful drafting, seeking legal advice, and ensuring that all parties have a clear understanding of the terms before entering into the contract.

4.2 Delay Tactics and Procedural Loopholes

Delay tactics and procedural loopholes are strategies used by parties involved in legal proceedings to prolong the resolution of a case or exploit weaknesses in the legal system. These tactics are often employed to gain an advantage or buy time, and can result in significant delays and increased costs for all parties involved. In the Indian legal system, delay tactics and procedural loopholes are not uncommon.

Some common examples include:

1. Filing frivolous applications: Parties may file unnecessary applications or motions to delay the proceedings. These applications may seek adjournments, request additional time for filing documents, or challenge the jurisdiction of the court.

2. Seeking frequent adjournments: Parties may request adjournments on various grounds, such as the unavailability of their lawyer, the need for additional time to prepare, or the absence of a key witness. These adjournments can cause significant delays in the progress of the case.

3. Misusing the process of discovery: Discovery is a legal process that allows parties to obtain information and evidence from each other. Parties may misuse this process by making excessive and irrelevant requests for documents or information, causing delays and increasing the workload for the opposing party.

4. Filing multiple appeals and revisions: Parties dissatisfied with a court's decision may file multiple appeals or revisions, which can further prolong the resolution of the case. These appeals and revisions may be filed on technical grounds or by challenging the interpretation of the law.

5. Exploiting procedural loopholes: Parties may exploit procedural loopholes to delay the proceedings. For example, they may challenge the validity of the service of summons, raise jurisdictional issues, or file applications for transfer of the case to another court.

To address these delay tactics and procedural loopholes, the Indian legal system has implemented various measures.

These include the imposition of costs for frivolous applications, strict timelines for filing documents and completing proceedings, and the use of alternative dispute resolution mechanisms like mediation and arbitration to expedite the resolution of disputes. However, despite these measures, delay tactics and procedural loopholes continue to be a challenge in the Indian legal system. Efforts are ongoing to streamline procedures, improve case management, and enhance the efficiency of the judiciary to minimize delays and ensure timely justice.

4.3 Ineffective Enforcement of Judgments

In India, the enforcement of judgments is governed by the Code of Civil Procedure, 1908. However, there have been concerns about the ineffective enforcement of judgments in the country. One of the main reasons for the ineffective enforcement of judgments is the backlog of cases in Indian courts. The Indian judicial system is burdened with a large number of pending cases, which leads to delays in the enforcement of judgments. This backlog is primarily due to the shortage of judges and infrastructure in the courts.

Another reason for the ineffective enforcement of judgments is the lack of coordination between different agencies involved in the enforcement process. There is often a lack of communication and coordination between the courts, the police, and other enforcement agencies, which hampers the timely execution of judgments. Additionally, there are instances where the parties against whom the judgment is passed intentionally evade the enforcement process. They may transfer their assets or take other measures to avoid complying with the judgment. This makes it difficult for the enforcement authorities to seize and sell the assets of the judgment debtor. Furthermore, the lack of awareness and understanding of the enforcement process among the general public also contributes to the ineffective enforcement of judgments.

Many people are not aware of their rights and the procedures involved in enforcing a judgment, which leads to a lack of cooperation and compliance. To address these issues, the Indian government has taken some steps to improve the enforcement of judgments. For example, the introduction of e-courts and online case management systems aims to reduce the backlog of cases and improve the efficiency of the judicial system. The government has also proposed amendments to the Code of Civil Procedure to streamline the enforcement process. However, despite these efforts, the enforcement of judgments in India continues to face challenges. It requires a comprehensive approach involving reforms in the judicial system, strengthening of enforcement agencies, and increasing awareness among the public to ensure effective enforcement of judgments.

4.4 Arbitration and Mediation Loopholes

Arbitration and mediation are alternative dispute resolution methods that are commonly used in India to resolve conflicts outside of the traditional court system. While these methods can be effective in providing a quicker and more cost-effective resolution to disputes, there are some loopholes that can be exploited by parties involved. Some of these loopholes include:

1. Lack of enforceability: Although arbitration awards are generally binding, there have been instances where parties have found ways to challenge or delay the enforcement of these awards. This can be done by questioning the validity of the arbitration agreement or by challenging the jurisdiction of the arbitral tribunal.

2. Lack of transparency: Unlike court proceedings, arbitration and mediation are private and confidential processes. While this can be beneficial in maintaining confidentiality, it can also create a lack of transparency, making it difficult for third parties to assess the fairness and impartiality of the proceedings.

3. Limited remedies: Arbitration and mediation may not provide the same range of remedies as a court judgment. For example, punitive damages or specific performance may not be available in arbitration or mediation, limiting the options for parties seeking redress.

4. Unequal bargaining power: In some cases, one party may have significantly more bargaining power than the other, leading to an imbalance in the negotiation process. This can result in unfair outcomes, where the weaker party is forced to accept unfavorable terms.

5. Lack of expertise: Arbitrators and mediators are typically chosen by the parties involved, and their expertise and qualifications can vary. In some cases, parties may select arbitrators or mediators who lack the necessary knowledge or experience to effectively resolve the dispute, leading to suboptimal outcomes.

6. Limited scope of review: The grounds for challenging arbitration awards are limited under Indian law. This can

make it difficult for parties to challenge an award, even if they believe that the arbitrator has made a mistake or acted in bad faith. It is important for parties considering arbitration or mediation to be aware of these loopholes and take steps to mitigate the risks associated with them. This can include carefully drafting arbitration agreements, selecting qualified arbitrators or mediators, and seeking legal advice throughout the process.

4.5 Fraud and Misrepresentation in Civil Cases

Fraud and misrepresentation are two important concepts in civil cases, particularly in the context of contract law. Both involve the intentional deception or misleading of another party, but they differ in certain aspects. Fraud refers to the deliberate misrepresentation of a material fact with the intention to deceive another party and induce them to act in a certain way.

In civil cases, fraud can occur in various forms, such as false statements, concealment of facts, or making promises with no intention to fulfill them. To establish fraud, the following elements must generally be proven:

1. Misrepresentation: The defendant made a false statement of fact or concealed a material fact.

2. Knowledge of falsity: The defendant knew that the statement was false or had no reasonable basis to believe it was true.

3. Intent to deceive: The defendant made the false statement with the intention to deceive the plaintiff.

4. Reliance: The plaintiff reasonably relied on the false statement and suffered harm as a result.

5. Damages: The plaintiff suffered actual damages or losses due to the fraud.

Misrepresentation, on the other hand, involves making false statements or representations that induce another party to enter into a contract or take some action. Unlike fraud, misrepresentation does not require proof of intent to deceive. There are three types of misrepresentation:

1. Innocent misrepresentation: The defendant made a false statement, but genuinely believed it to be true.

2. Negligent misrepresentation: The defendant made a false statement without exercising reasonable care to ensure its accuracy.

3. Fraudulent misrepresentation: The defendant made a false statement knowingly or recklessly, without any reasonable belief in its truth.

In civil cases, the remedies available for fraud and misrepresentation may include rescission of the contract, damages, or specific performance. It is important to note that the burden of proof lies with the party alleging fraud or misrepresentation, and they must provide sufficient evidence to establish their claims. It is advisable to consult with a legal professional or refer to specific laws and regulations in your jurisdiction to understand the exact requirements and procedures related to fraud and misrepresentation in civil cases.

Chapter 5:
Constitutional Law Loopholes

Constitutional law loopholes refer to gaps or ambiguities in the language or interpretation of a constitution that allow for certain actions or practices that may not align with the original intent or spirit of the constitution. These loopholes can be exploited by individuals, groups, or even the government to bypass or circumvent constitutional provisions.

In the context of Indian constitutional law, there have been instances where loopholes have been identified and exploited. Some examples include:

1. Reservation Policies: The Indian Constitution provides for reservation of seats in educational institutions and government jobs for certain disadvantaged groups. However, there have been instances where the criteria for determining eligibility for reservation have been manipulated or misused, leading to the exclusion of deserving candidates or the inclusion of those who may not be genuinely disadvantaged.

2. Emergency Provisions: The Indian Constitution allows for the declaration of a state of emergency in certain circumstances, such as during war or internal disturbances. However, there have been instances where emergency provisions have been misused by the government to

suppress dissent or curtail fundamental rights, going beyond the intended scope of the constitution.

3. Judicial Interpretation: The interpretation of constitutional provisions by the judiciary can sometimes create loopholes. Different interpretations by different courts can lead to conflicting judgments and inconsistent application of the law. This can result in uncertainty and exploitation of these loopholes by individuals or entities seeking to evade legal obligations or exploit legal loopholes.

4. Legislative Loopholes: The drafting of legislation can sometimes leave room for interpretation or exploitation. Ambiguities or gaps in the language of laws can be exploited by individuals or entities to circumvent legal requirements or obligations.

It is important to note that the identification and exploitation of constitutional law loopholes can have significant implications for the functioning of a democratic society. It can undermine the rule of law, erode public trust in institutions, and lead to unequal treatment or injustice. Therefore, it is crucial for lawmakers, the judiciary, and citizens to be vigilant and address these loopholes through legal reforms and robust enforcement mechanisms.

5.1 Fundamental Rights and their Limitations

Fundamental Rights are a set of basic rights and freedoms that are guaranteed to all citizens of India under Part III of the Indian Constitution. These rights are considered essential for the overall development and well-being of individuals and are enforceable by the courts. However, these rights are not absolute and are subject to certain limitations. The limitations on fundamental rights are imposed to maintain public order, protect the interests of the state, and ensure the welfare of the society as a whole. Some of the limitations on fundamental rights are as follows:

1. Reasonable restrictions: The Constitution allows for the imposition of reasonable restrictions on the exercise of fundamental rights in the interest of public order, morality, security, and the sovereignty and integrity of India. These restrictions must be reasonable and cannot be arbitrary or excessive.

2. Public emergency: During a period of emergency, certain fundamental rights can be suspended or restricted. The President can declare a state of emergency in case of war, external aggression, or armed rebellion. However, the right to life and personal liberty cannot be suspended even during an emergency.

3. Protection of interests of Scheduled Castes, Scheduled Tribes, and other backward classes: The Constitution provides for affirmative action to protect the interests of these marginalized communities. Special provisions can be made to promote their social, educational, and economic advancement, even if it restricts the rights of others.

4. Protection of public interest: Fundamental rights can be limited to protect the larger public interest. For example, the right to freedom of speech and expression can be restricted to prevent hate speech, defamation, or incitement to violence.

5. Restrictions on government employees: Fundamental rights can be restricted for government employees to ensure

the proper functioning of the administration. For example, restrictions can be imposed on their right to freedom of speech and expression to maintain discipline and confidentiality.

It is important to note that any restriction on fundamental rights must be reasonable, proportionate, and in accordance with the principles of natural justice. The courts play a crucial role in interpreting and balancing the exercise of fundamental rights with their limitations to ensure a fair and just society.

5.2 Judicial Activism and Interpretation

Judicial activism refers to the tendency of judges to interpret and apply the law in a way that goes beyond the traditional role of the judiciary. It involves judges taking an active role in shaping public policy and making decisions that have a significant impact on society.

In the context of Indian laws, judicial activism has played a crucial role in shaping the legal landscape of the country. The Indian judiciary, particularly the Supreme Court, has been known for its proactive approach in interpreting and expanding the scope of fundamental rights guaranteed by the Constitution. One of the key aspects of judicial activism in India is the interpretation of the Constitution. The Supreme Court has often interpreted the provisions of the Constitution in a broad and progressive manner, in order to protect and promote the rights of citizens.

For example, the Court has expanded the definition of the right to life to include the right to clean environment, right to privacy, and right to dignity. Judicial activism in India has also been evident in the areas of social justice and public interest litigation (PIL). The Supreme Court has taken up several PIL cases, where it has intervened to address issues of public importance and protect the rights of marginalized sections of society. This has led to significant changes in areas such as environmental protection, women's rights, and the rights of the LGBTQ+ community.

However, judicial activism has also been a subject of criticism. Critics argue that it encroaches upon the domain of the legislature and executive, and undermines the principle of separation of powers. They argue that judges should limit themselves to interpreting the law, rather than making policy decisions.

In conclusion, judicial activism in India has played a crucial role in shaping the legal landscape and protecting the rights of citizens. While it has been instrumental in bringing about social change and addressing issues of public importance, it has also been a subject of debate and criticism.

5.3 Legislative Overreach and Constitutional Amendments

Legislative overreach refers to a situation where the legislature exceeds its constitutional authority by enacting laws that go beyond its prescribed powers. It occurs when the legislature encroaches upon the powers of other branches of government or violates the fundamental rights of individuals. Constitutional amendments, on the other hand, are changes made to the constitution of a country. These amendments are usually made to adapt the constitution to changing times, address societal needs, or correct any deficiencies in the original constitution.

In the context of Indian laws, legislative overreach can occur when the legislature enacts laws that are inconsistent with the provisions of the Constitution of India. The Constitution of India is the supreme law of the land and any law that violates its provisions can be struck down by the judiciary as unconstitutional. Constitutional amendments in India are governed by Article 368 of the Constitution. The procedure for amending the constitution is laid down in this article, which requires a special majority in both houses of Parliament.

However, there have been instances where constitutional amendments have been challenged in court on the grounds of violating the basic structure of the constitution. The concept of legislative overreach and constitutional amendments is important in maintaining the balance of power between the different branches of government and protecting the fundamental rights of individuals. It ensures that the legislature does not exceed its authority and that any changes to the constitution are made in accordance with the prescribed procedure and do not undermine the basic structure of the constitution.

5.4 Reservation Policies and Affirmative Action

Reservation policies and affirmative action are two important aspects of Indian laws that aim to address historical social and economic inequalities and promote equal opportunities for marginalized and disadvantaged groups. Reservation policies in India refer to the system of reserving a certain percentage of seats or positions in educational institutions, government jobs, and legislative bodies for Scheduled Castes (SC), Scheduled Tribes (ST), and Other Backward Classes (OBC). These groups have historically faced discrimination and social exclusion, and reservation policies are intended to provide them with opportunities for education, employment, and political representation.

Affirmative action, on the other hand, is a broader concept that encompasses various measures taken to promote equal opportunities and representation for marginalized groups. It includes not only reservation policies but also initiatives such as scholarships, financial aid, and special provisions for women, persons with disabilities, and religious minorities. The reservation policies in India are governed by the Constitution of India, which provides for the reservation of seats for SCs, STs, and OBCs in educational institutions and government jobs. The percentage of reservation varies from state to state and is determined by the government based on the population of these groups in each state. Affirmative action and reservation policies have been a subject of debate and controversy in India. While proponents argue that these policies are necessary to address historical injustices and promote social equality, critics argue that they perpetuate caste-based divisions and hinder meritocracy.

Over the years, there have been calls for revisiting and reforming reservation policies to ensure that they are more inclusive and effective in achieving their objectives. Efforts have also been made to extend reservation benefits to economically weaker sections of society, irrespective of caste or religion. Overall, reservation policies and affirmative action in India are aimed at promoting social justice, equal opportunities, and inclusive development.

However, the effectiveness and impact of these policies continue to be debated, and there is a need for ongoing evaluation and reform to ensure their relevance and fairness in a rapidly changing society.

5.5 Freedom of Speech and Expression

Freedom of speech and expression is a fundamental right guaranteed to every citizen of India under Article 19(1)(a) of the Constitution of India. This right allows individuals to express their thoughts, opinions, beliefs, and ideas freely without any fear of censorship or punishment by the government. However, this right is not absolute and is subject to certain reasonable restrictions imposed by the State. These restrictions are mentioned under Article 19(2) and include concerns such as public order, decency, morality, security of the state, defamation, incitement to an offense, and contempt of court.

The Supreme Court of India has played a crucial role in interpreting and safeguarding the freedom of speech and expression. It has consistently held that this right is essential for the functioning of a democratic society and is a cornerstone of individual liberty. The court has also emphasized the importance of protecting unpopular and controversial opinions, as they contribute to the marketplace of ideas and promote a healthy democracy. However, there have been instances where the freedom of speech and expression has been curtailed or misused. The government has the power to impose reasonable restrictions to maintain public order and protect the interests of the nation. In recent years, there have been debates and controversies surrounding issues such as hate speech, sedition, online censorship, and restrictions on artistic freedom.

Overall, while the freedom of speech and expression is a fundamental right in India, it is important to strike a balance between protecting this right and ensuring that it does not infringe upon the rights and interests of others or pose a threat to public order and national security.

Chapter 6:
Administrative Law Loopholes

Administrative law refers to the body of law that governs the actions and decisions of administrative agencies, which are government bodies responsible for implementing and enforcing laws and regulations. While administrative law aims to ensure transparency, accountability, and fairness in administrative decision-making, there can be loopholes or shortcomings in its implementation.

Some common administrative law loopholes include:

1. Lack of procedural safeguards: Administrative agencies may not always follow proper procedures when making decisions, such as providing notice and an opportunity to be heard to affected parties. This can lead to arbitrary or unfair decisions.

2. Insufficient oversight and accountability: Administrative agencies may lack effective oversight mechanisms, allowing them to act with impunity. This can result in abuse of power, corruption, or biased decision-making.

3. Delayed or inadequate remedies: Administrative law often provides for remedies, such as appeals or judicial review, to challenge administrative decisions. However, these remedies may be slow, costly, or ineffective, making it difficult for affected parties to seek redress.

4. Inconsistent interpretation and application of laws: Different administrative agencies or officials may interpret and apply laws differently, leading to inconsistencies and confusion. This can create opportunities for exploitation or manipulation of the law.

5. Regulatory capture: Administrative agencies may become influenced or controlled by the industries or interest groups they are supposed to regulate. This can result in biased decision-making that favors certain stakeholders over others.

6. Lack of transparency: Administrative agencies may not always provide sufficient information or reasons for their decisions, making it difficult for affected parties to understand or challenge those decisions.

7. Limited public participation: Administrative decision-making processes may not always allow for meaningful public participation, limiting the input and influence of affected individuals or communities.

Addressing these loopholes requires ongoing efforts to strengthen administrative law and its implementation. This can include reforms such as enhancing procedural safeguards, improving oversight mechanisms, promoting transparency and accountability, and increasing public participation in administrative decision-making processes.

6.1 Administrative Discretion and Abuse of Power

Administrative discretion refers to the authority given to administrative agencies or officials to make decisions and take actions within their designated areas of responsibility. It allows them to exercise judgment and flexibility in implementing laws and regulations. However, the exercise of administrative discretion is not unlimited, and there is a potential for abuse of power.

Abuse of power occurs when administrative officials misuse their authority for personal gain, to discriminate against certain individuals or groups, or to act in a manner that is arbitrary, capricious, or contrary to the principles of fairness and justice.

In India, administrative discretion is subject to certain legal principles and safeguards to prevent abuse of power. These include:

1. Rule of law: Administrative actions must be in accordance with the law and cannot be arbitrary or unreasonable.

2. Procedural fairness: Administrative decisions must be made after giving affected parties an opportunity to be heard and present their case.

3. Reasoned decision-making: Administrative decisions should be based on relevant facts, evidence, and reasons, and should not be influenced by irrelevant considerations.

4. Non-discrimination: Administrative officials must not discriminate against individuals or groups based on factors such as race, religion, gender, or caste.

5. Judicial review: Administrative actions can be challenged in courts to ensure that they are within the scope of the law and do not involve abuse of power.

6. Ombudsman: The institution of the ombudsman provides a mechanism for individuals to lodge complaints against

administrative officials and seek redress for any abuse of power.

Despite these safeguards, instances of abuse of power by administrative officials can still occur. It is important for individuals to be aware of their rights and recourse mechanisms, and for the government to ensure transparency, accountability, and effective oversight of administrative actions to prevent and address any abuse of power.

6.2 Lack of Transparency and Accountability

Lack of transparency and accountability is a major issue in the Indian legal system. This problem is prevalent at various levels, including the legislative, executive, and judicial branches of the government. In the legislative branch, there is often a lack of transparency in the law-making process. Bills are sometimes introduced without proper public consultation or debate, and important decisions are made behind closed doors. This lack of transparency undermines the democratic principles of accountability and public participation.

Similarly, the executive branch also suffers from a lack of transparency and accountability. Government officials often make decisions without proper justification or explanation, and there is a lack of transparency in the allocation of resources and implementation of policies. This lack of accountability leads to corruption and misuse of public funds.

The judicial branch, which is supposed to be the guardian of transparency and accountability, also faces challenges in this regard. There have been instances of corruption and nepotism within the judiciary, which erode public trust in the system. Additionally, the lack of transparency in the appointment and promotion of judges raises concerns about the independence and impartiality of the judiciary.

The lack of transparency and accountability in the Indian legal system has serious consequences for the rule of law and the protection of citizens' rights. It allows for the abuse of power, undermines public trust in the government, and hampers the effective functioning of the justice system. Efforts have been made to address these issues, such as the Right to Information Act, which aims to promote transparency and accountability in government institutions.

However, more needs to be done to ensure that transparency and accountability are upheld at all levels of the legal system. This includes strengthening mechanisms for public participation, promoting a culture of openness and accountability among government officials, and ensuring the independence and integrity of the judiciary.

6.3 Red Tape and Bureaucratic Delays

Red tape and bureaucratic delays refer to the excessive and unnecessary bureaucratic procedures and paperwork that can hinder the efficient functioning of government processes and delay decision-making. In the context of Indian laws, red tape and bureaucratic delays are often cited as major challenges that individuals and businesses face when dealing with government agencies and institutions. India has a complex and extensive legal framework, with numerous laws, regulations, and procedures governing various aspects of life and business. While these laws are intended to ensure transparency, accountability, and fairness, the implementation and enforcement of these laws often suffer from bureaucratic inefficiencies and delays.

One of the main reasons for red tape and bureaucratic delays in India is the excessive paperwork and documentation required for various government processes. Individuals and businesses often have to navigate through multiple layers of bureaucracy, submit numerous forms and documents, and wait for extended periods for approvals and clearances. This can lead to significant delays and frustration, especially for those seeking timely resolution of legal matters or starting and running a business.

Another contributing factor to red tape and bureaucratic delays is the lack of coordination and communication between different government departments and agencies. Often, multiple departments are involved in the decision-making process, and the lack of effective coordination can lead to confusion, duplication of efforts, and delays in obtaining necessary approvals.

Corruption and bribery also play a role in exacerbating red tape and bureaucratic delays in India. Individuals and businesses may be forced to pay bribes or engage in corrupt practices to expedite processes or bypass bureaucratic hurdles. This not only perpetuates a culture of corruption but also further slows down the system and undermines the rule of law.

Efforts have been made by the Indian government to address these issues. Initiatives such as digitization of government processes, simplification of procedures, and the introduction of online portals for various services aim to reduce red tape and bureaucratic delays. However, there is still a long way to go in streamlining the legal system and improving the efficiency of government processes to ensure timely and effective implementation of Indian laws.

6.4 Public Interest Litigation and its Misuse

Public Interest Litigation (PIL) is a legal mechanism in India that allows any citizen or organization to file a petition in the court on behalf of the public interest. It is a tool to ensure that justice is accessible to all and to address issues that affect a large section of society. However, like any legal provision, PIL can be misused. Some of the common ways in which PIL is misused are:

1. Personal vendetta: PIL can be filed with malicious intent to settle personal scores or harass individuals or organizations. This misuse undermines the purpose of PIL and wastes the court's time and resources.

2. Frivolous petitions: Some PILs are filed without any genuine public interest involved. These petitions may be filed for publicity or to gain personal benefits. Such petitions clog the court system and divert attention from genuine issues.

3. Delaying tactics: PILs can be misused as a means to delay or obstruct development projects or government policies. By filing PILs, individuals or groups can create hurdles and cause unnecessary delays, leading to increased costs and inefficiencies.

4. Political motives: PILs can be used as a tool by political parties or individuals to target their opponents or gain political mileage. Such petitions may not genuinely serve

the public interest but are filed to create a negative perception or disrupt the functioning of the government.

5. Lack of accountability: In some cases, PILs are filed without proper research or evidence, leading to baseless allegations and unnecessary litigation. This lack of accountability can result in the misuse of PILs and cause harm to individuals or organizations.

To address the issue of misuse, the courts have taken steps to discourage frivolous PILs. The Supreme Court has imposed fines on petitioners who file frivolous or vexatious PILs. Additionally, the courts have become more cautious in admitting PILs and have laid down guidelines to ensure that only genuine public interest matters are entertained. It is important to strike a balance between the right to access justice and preventing the misuse of PILs. While PILs play a crucial role in safeguarding public interest, steps should be taken to prevent their misuse and ensure that they serve their intended purpose.

6.5 Environmental Regulations and Compliance

Environmental regulations and compliance in India are governed by various laws and regulations. Some of the key laws and regulations related to environmental protection and compliance in India include:

1. The Water (Prevention and Control of Pollution) Act, 1974: This act aims to prevent and control water pollution by regulating the discharge of pollutants into water bodies and establishing pollution control boards at the central and state levels.

2. The Air (Prevention and Control of Pollution) Act, 1981: This act aims to prevent and control air pollution by regulating the emission of pollutants from industries, vehicles, and other sources. It also establishes pollution control boards at the central and state levels.

3. The Environment (Protection) Act, 1986: This act provides for the protection and improvement of the environment and the prevention of hazards to human beings, other living creatures, plants, and property. It empowers the central government to take measures to protect and improve the environment and sets out penalties for violations.

4. The Forest (Conservation) Act, 1980: This act regulates the diversion of forest land for non-forest purposes and requires prior approval from the central government for such diversion. It aims to ensure the conservation and sustainable management of forests.

5. The Hazardous and Other Wastes (Management and Transboundary Movement) Rules, 2016: These rules regulate the management and disposal of hazardous and other wastes. They require waste generators to take measures for the safe handling, storage, transportation, and disposal of such wastes.

6. The Wildlife Protection Act, 1972: This act provides for the protection and conservation of wildlife in India. It prohibits hunting, poaching, and trade in wildlife and their products, and establishes protected areas and wildlife sanctuaries.

Compliance with these laws and regulations is enforced by various authorities, including the Central Pollution Control Board (CPCB) and State Pollution Control Boards (SPCBs), which have the power to issue directions, conduct inspections, and impose penalties for non-compliance. Non-compliance with environmental regulations can result in fines, closure of operations, or imprisonment, depending on the severity of the violation.

Chapter 7:
Intellectual Property Law Loopholes

Intellectual property law loopholes refer to gaps or weaknesses in the legal framework that can be exploited to circumvent or undermine the protection of intellectual property rights. These loopholes can be used by individuals or companies to avoid legal consequences for infringing on someone else's intellectual property or to gain an unfair advantage in the market.

Some common intellectual property law loopholes include:

1. Parallel imports: This refers to the practice of importing genuine products from one country to another without the authorization of the intellectual property rights holder. Parallel imports exploit price differences between countries and can undermine the rights holder's ability to control the distribution and pricing of their products.

2. Patent trolls: Patent trolls are individuals or companies that acquire patents solely for the purpose of suing or threatening to sue others for patent infringement. They exploit weaknesses in the patent system, such as vague or overly broad patents, to extract licensing fees or settlements from alleged infringers.

3. Copyright infringement on the internet: The internet has made it easier to copy and distribute copyrighted material without permission. Loopholes in copyright law, such as safe harbor provisions for internet service providers, can

make it difficult for rights holders to enforce their copyrights online.

4. Trade secret theft: Trade secrets are valuable business information that is kept confidential. Loopholes in trade secret laws can make it challenging for companies to protect their trade secrets from theft or misappropriation, especially when employees or business partners are involved.

5. Reverse engineering: Reverse engineering involves analyzing and disassembling a product to understand its design or functionality. While reverse engineering is generally legal, it can be used to copy or replicate patented inventions or copyrighted works without permission. It is important to note that these loopholes may vary in different jurisdictions, and laws are constantly evolving to address these issues.

Intellectual property rights holders should stay informed about the latest legal developments and take appropriate measures to protect their intellectual property.

7.1 Patent and Copyright Infringement

Patent and copyright infringement are two different types of intellectual property violations.

Patent Infringement: A patent is a legal protection granted to an inventor for their invention, giving them exclusive rights to make, use, and sell their invention for a limited period of time. Patent infringement occurs when someone uses, makes, sells, or imports a patented invention without the permission of the patent holder. This can include manufacturing, selling, or using a product or process that is covered by a valid patent. Patent infringement can result in legal action, and the patent holder may seek damages or an injunction to stop the infringing activity.

Copyright Infringement: Copyright is a legal protection granted to the creators of original works, such as literary, artistic, musical, or dramatic works. Copyright infringement occurs when someone uses, reproduces, distributes, or displays a copyrighted work without the permission of the copyright owner. This can include copying, distributing, or performing a copyrighted work without authorization. Copyright infringement can also result in legal action, and the copyright owner may seek damages or an injunction to stop the infringing activity.

In India, patent infringement is governed by the Patents Act, 1970, while copyright infringement is governed by the Copyright Act, 1957. Both acts provide remedies and penalties for infringement, including damages, injunctions, and criminal prosecution in some cases. It is important for individuals and businesses to respect and protect intellectual property rights to avoid legal consequences.

7.2 Trademark and Trade Secret Violations

Trademark and trade secret violations are two different types of intellectual property infringements.

Trademark Violations: A trademark is a distinctive sign or symbol that identifies and distinguishes the goods or services of one party from those of others. Trademark violations occur when someone uses a trademark without the owner's permission, leading to confusion among consumers or dilution of the trademark's distinctiveness.

Some common types of trademark violations include:

1. Trademark Infringement: This occurs when someone uses a trademark that is identical or similar to an existing registered trademark for similar goods or services, causing confusion among consumers.

2. Trademark Counterfeiting: This involves the unauthorized use of a trademark on counterfeit goods, which are then sold as genuine products, deceiving consumers and harming the reputation of the trademark owner.

3. Trademark Dilution: This occurs when someone uses a famous trademark in a way that weakens its distinctiveness or tarnishes its reputation, even if there is no likelihood of confusion.

Trade Secret Violations: A trade secret is confidential and proprietary information that provides a competitive advantage to a business. Trade secret violations occur when someone acquires, uses, or discloses another party's trade secret without authorization.

Some common types of trade secret violations include:

1. Misappropriation: This involves the unauthorized acquisition, use, or disclosure of a trade secret by someone who has a duty to keep it confidential, such as an employee or a business partner.

2. Industrial Espionage: This refers to the deliberate and unlawful acquisition of trade secrets through spying, hacking, or other illegal means.

3. Breach of Confidentiality Agreements: This occurs when someone violates a contractual obligation to keep trade secrets confidential, such as by sharing the information with unauthorized parties.

In India, trademark violations are governed by the Trade Marks Act, 1999, while trade secret violations are addressed under the Indian Contract Act, 1872, and the Information Technology Act, 2000. Legal remedies for trademark and trade secret violations may include injunctions, damages, account of profits, and other appropriate relief as determined by the courts.

7.3 Piracy and Counterfeiting

Piracy and counterfeiting refer to the illegal reproduction, distribution, or sale of copyrighted materials or counterfeit goods. These activities are considered intellectual property rights violations and are subject to legal action in many countries, including India.

In India, piracy and counterfeiting are addressed under various laws and regulations, including the Copyright Act, 1957, the Trademarks Act, 1999, and the Indian Penal Code, 1860.

Under the Copyright Act, piracy refers to the unauthorized reproduction, distribution, or public performance of copyrighted works, such as books, music, films, software, etc. The act provides for civil and criminal remedies against piracy, including injunctions, damages, and imprisonment.

Counterfeiting, on the other hand, involves the unauthorized production, distribution, or sale of goods that bear a trademark or trade dress that is identical or deceptively similar to a registered trademark. The Trademarks Act provides for civil and criminal remedies against counterfeiting, including injunctions, damages, and imprisonment. In addition to these specific laws, the Indian Penal Code also contains provisions that can be used to address piracy and counterfeiting.

For example, Section 63 of the Indian Penal Code deals with the punishment for counterfeiting a trade mark, while Section 63A deals with the punishment for selling goods with a counterfeit trademark.

To combat piracy and counterfeiting, the Indian government has established specialized enforcement agencies, such as the Economic Offences Wing (EOW) and the Central Bureau of Investigation (CBI), which work in coordination with the police and other authorities to investigate and prosecute offenders. It is important to note that piracy and counterfeiting not only harm the rights holders but also have significant economic and social implications. They undermine legitimate businesses, deprive creators of their rightful income, and can pose risks to consumer health and safety. Therefore, it is crucial to raise awareness about the importance of respecting intellectual property rights and to enforce the laws effectively to deter piracy and counterfeiting activities.

7.4 Challenges in Enforcement and Protection

Enforcement and protection of laws in India face several challenges. Some of the key challenges include:

1. Lack of awareness: Many people in India are not aware of their rights and the laws that protect them. This lack of

awareness makes it difficult for individuals to seek legal recourse and for law enforcement agencies to effectively enforce the laws.

2. Corruption: Corruption is a major challenge in the enforcement and protection of laws in India. Bribery and other forms of corruption can hinder the proper implementation of laws and undermine the justice system.

3. Inadequate resources: Law enforcement agencies often face a lack of resources, including manpower, equipment, and infrastructure. This can hamper their ability to effectively enforce laws and protect individuals.

4. Delayed justice: The Indian legal system is notorious for its slow pace, leading to delayed justice. This delay can discourage individuals from seeking legal remedies and can also result in a lack of faith in the justice system.

5. Gender bias: Gender bias is a significant challenge in the enforcement and protection of laws in India, particularly in cases of violence against women. Many cases of gender-based violence go unreported or are not taken seriously by law enforcement agencies.

6. Inefficient legal processes: The legal processes in India can be complex and time-consuming. This can make it difficult for individuals to navigate the legal system and seek justice.

7. Lack of coordination: There is often a lack of coordination between different law enforcement agencies and departments, leading to inefficiencies in the enforcement and protection of laws.

8. Social and cultural barriers: Social and cultural norms can act as barriers to the enforcement and protection of laws.

For example, caste-based discrimination and honor killings are challenges that the legal system faces in India. Addressing these challenges requires a multi-faceted approach, including raising awareness, improving resources and infrastructure, tackling corruption, and implementing legal reforms to expedite the justice system.

7.5 International Intellectual Property Law Discrepancies

International intellectual property law discrepancies refer to the differences and inconsistencies that exist between the intellectual property laws of different countries. These discrepancies can create challenges and complexities for individuals and businesses seeking to protect their intellectual property rights globally.

One major discrepancy in international intellectual property law is the varying levels of protection and enforcement provided by different countries. Some countries have robust intellectual property laws and strong enforcement mechanisms, while others may have weaker laws or lack the resources to effectively enforce them. This can lead to disparities in the level of protection afforded to intellectual property rights holders in different jurisdictions.

Another discrepancy is the differences in the scope and duration of intellectual property rights. For example, copyright laws may vary in terms of what works are eligible for protection, the duration of protection, and the rights and limitations granted to copyright holders.

Similarly, patent laws may differ in terms of the criteria for patentability, the scope of patent rights, and the duration of patent protection. The procedures and requirements for obtaining and maintaining intellectual property rights also vary across countries.

For example, the process for registering a trademark or filing a patent application may differ in terms of the documentation required, the examination process, and the fees involved. These differences can create challenges for individuals and businesses seeking to protect their intellectual property rights globally.

Discrepancies in international intellectual property law can also arise in the context of cross-border disputes and enforcement actions. Differences in legal systems, court procedures, and remedies available can complicate the resolution of intellectual property disputes that span multiple jurisdictions. Efforts have been made to harmonize and standardize international intellectual property laws through international treaties and agreements.

Examples include the World Intellectual Property Organization (WIPO) treaties, such as the Berne Convention for the Protection of Literary and Artistic Works and the Paris Convention for the Protection of Industrial Property. These treaties aim to establish minimum standards of protection and facilitate the international recognition and enforcement of intellectual property rights. However, despite these efforts, discrepancies in international intellectual property law persist, and navigating the global intellectual property landscape remains a complex task for individuals and businesses.

It is important for intellectual property rights holders to understand the legal framework and requirements in each jurisdiction where they seek protection, and to work with legal professionals who specialize in international intellectual property law to navigate these discrepancies effectively.

Chapter 8:
Taxation Law Loopholes

Taxation law loopholes refer to legal ways that individuals or businesses can exploit to minimize their tax liability or avoid paying taxes altogether. These loopholes are often created due to ambiguities or gaps in the tax laws, allowing taxpayers to take advantage of certain provisions or structures to reduce their tax burden.

Some common examples of taxation law loopholes include:

1. Offshore tax havens: Individuals or businesses can establish offshore accounts or entities in countries with low or no tax rates to shelter their income or assets from taxation.

2. Transfer pricing: Multinational corporations can manipulate the prices of goods or services transferred between their subsidiaries in different countries to shift profits to low-tax jurisdictions.

3. Tax deductions and credits: Taxpayers can take advantage of various deductions and credits available under the tax laws to reduce their taxable income or offset their tax liability.

4. Tax shelters: Certain investments or financial structures, such as real estate partnerships or energy tax credits, can be used to generate losses or tax credits that can be used to offset taxable income.

5. Trusts and estate planning: Individuals can use trusts or other estate planning strategies to transfer assets to future generations while minimizing the tax consequences.

It is important to note that while some tax planning strategies may be legal, aggressive or abusive tax avoidance schemes can be considered illegal and may result in penalties or legal consequences. Tax authorities are constantly working to close these loopholes and prevent tax evasion.

8.1 Tax Evasion and Avoidance Strategies

Tax evasion and tax avoidance are two different concepts, with tax evasion being illegal and tax avoidance being legal. Here are some strategies commonly used for tax evasion and tax avoidance:

Tax Evasion Strategies:

1. Underreporting Income: Individuals or businesses may intentionally fail to report their full income to the tax authorities.

2. Overstating Deductions: Taxpayers may inflate their deductions or claim false expenses to reduce their taxable income.

3. Offshore Tax Havens: Individuals or businesses may hide their income or assets in offshore accounts to avoid paying taxes.

4. Shell Companies: Creating fictitious companies or using shell companies to hide income or assets from tax authorities.

5. False Invoices: Businesses may create false invoices or manipulate their accounting records to understate their income.

6. Cash Transactions: Engaging in cash transactions to avoid creating a paper trail and evade taxes.

Tax Avoidance Strategies:

1. Tax Planning: Legally structuring financial affairs to minimize tax liability by taking advantage of available deductions, exemptions, and credits.

2. Incorporation: Businesses may incorporate to take advantage of lower corporate tax rates or other tax benefits.

3. Tax-efficient Investments: Investing in tax-efficient instruments such as tax-free bonds, retirement accounts, or tax-exempt mutual funds.

4. Income Shifting: Transferring income to family members or entities with lower tax rates or utilizing income-splitting strategies.

5. Tax Treaties: Taking advantage of tax treaties between countries to reduce or eliminate double taxation.

6. Charitable Donations: Making donations to registered charities to claim deductions and reduce taxable income.

It is important to note that tax evasion is illegal and can result in severe penalties, including fines and imprisonment. Tax avoidance, on the other hand, is legal and is considered a legitimate way to minimize tax liability within the boundaries of the law.

8.2 Transfer Pricing and Shell Companies

Transfer pricing refers to the pricing of goods, services, or intangible assets transferred between related entities within a multinational enterprise (MNE). It involves determining the appropriate prices for such transactions to ensure that they are conducted at arm's length, meaning that the prices are similar to what would be charged between unrelated parties in a similar transaction.

Shell companies, on the other hand, are entities that are typically created for the purpose of holding assets or conducting business activities, but they often lack substantial operations or employees. These companies are often used for various purposes, including tax planning, asset protection, and hiding the true ownership of assets.

In the context of transfer pricing, shell companies can be used to manipulate prices and shift profits between related entities within an MNE. This can be done by artificially inflating or deflating the prices of goods, services, or intangible assets transferred between these entities. By doing so, the MNE can reduce its tax liability in certain jurisdictions or take advantage of more favorable tax regimes. To address the issue of transfer pricing manipulation through shell companies, many countries, including India, have implemented strict transfer pricing regulations. These regulations require MNEs to determine transfer prices based on the arm's length principle and provide detailed documentation to support their pricing decisions.

Additionally, tax authorities have the power to make transfer pricing adjustments if they believe that the prices charged in related-party transactions are not at arm's length. In India, the transfer pricing regulations are governed by the Income Tax Act, 1961, and the rules issued thereunder.

The Indian tax authorities have the power to make transfer pricing adjustments if they believe that the prices charged in related-party transactions are not at arm's length. They can also impose penalties and initiate prosecution for non-compliance with the transfer pricing regulations.

Overall, transfer pricing and shell companies are closely related as shell companies can be used as a tool to manipulate transfer prices and shift profits within an MNE. However, strict transfer pricing regulations aim to prevent such manipulation and ensure that related-party transactions are conducted at arm's length.

8.3 Black Money and Offshore Accounts

Black money refers to funds that are earned through illegal means or are not declared for tax purposes. It is often kept hidden from the government authorities to avoid paying taxes or to engage in illegal activities such as money laundering.

Offshore accounts, on the other hand, are bank accounts held in a foreign country by an individual or entity. These accounts are often used to store and manage funds outside of the individual's home country. Offshore accounts can be legal and legitimate, but they can also be used for illegal purposes such as hiding black money.

In India, the government has taken several measures to tackle the issue of black money and offshore accounts. The most notable initiative is the Black Money (Undisclosed

Foreign Income and Assets) and Imposition of Tax Act, 2015. This act provides a framework for dealing with undisclosed foreign income and assets, and imposes penalties and taxes on individuals who fail to disclose such income or assets. Under this act, individuals are required to disclose their foreign income and assets in their tax returns. Failure to do so can result in penalties and prosecution. The act also provides for the establishment of a special investigation team (SIT) to investigate cases of black money and offshore accounts. Additionally, the government has signed various tax information exchange agreements (TIEAs) and entered into bilateral tax treaties with several countries to facilitate the exchange of information on offshore accounts and black money.

Overall, the Indian government is committed to cracking down on black money and offshore accounts to promote transparency and ensure compliance with tax laws.

8.4 Double Taxation Agreements

Double Taxation Agreements (DTAs) are bilateral agreements between two countries that aim to eliminate the double taxation of income or capital gains that may arise when a taxpayer is a resident of one country but earns income or gains from another country.

These agreements are designed to promote cross-border trade and investment by providing relief from double taxation, ensuring that taxpayers are not taxed twice on the same income or gains. DTAs typically allocate taxing rights between the two countries, specify the methods for eliminating double taxation, and provide for the exchange of information between tax authorities.

The main objectives of DTAs are to:

1. Avoid double taxation: DTAs provide mechanisms to avoid or mitigate the impact of double taxation on individuals and businesses. This is achieved by either exempting certain types of income from taxation in one country or providing a tax credit for taxes paid in the other country.

2. Promote cross-border trade and investment: By eliminating or reducing the tax barriers, DTAs encourage cross-border trade and investment by providing certainty and predictability to taxpayers. This helps in attracting foreign investment and promoting economic growth.

3. Prevent tax evasion and avoidance: DTAs include provisions for the exchange of information between tax authorities of the two countries. This helps in preventing tax evasion and avoidance by ensuring that taxpayers cannot hide income or assets in one country to avoid taxation in the other.

India has entered into DTAs with several countries to avoid double taxation and promote economic cooperation. These agreements cover various aspects such as taxation of income from employment, business profits, dividends, interest, royalties, capital gains, and other sources of income.

The agreements also provide for the resolution of disputes between the tax authorities of the two countries. DTAs play a crucial role in facilitating international trade and investment by providing a framework for fair and equitable taxation. They help in reducing tax burdens, eliminating barriers to cross-border transactions, and promoting economic cooperation between countries.

8.5 Taxation of Digital Economy

Taxation of the digital economy refers to the process of levying taxes on economic activities that are conducted through digital platforms or involve digital goods and services. With the rapid growth of the digital economy, governments around the world are grappling with the challenge of effectively taxing these activities.

In India, the taxation of the digital economy is governed by various laws and regulations. The primary legislation that deals with taxation in India is the Income Tax Act, 1961. Under this act, income generated from digital activities is subject to taxation. The Indian government has taken several measures to ensure that the digital economy is effectively taxed. One such measure is the introduction of the Equalization Levy, which was first introduced in 2016.

The Equalization Levy is a tax on specified digital services provided by non-resident companies to Indian residents. It is levied at a rate of 6% on the gross amount of consideration paid for these services. Additionally, the Indian government has also introduced the concept of a Permanent Establishment (PE) in the digital economy. A PE is a fixed place of business through which a non-resident company carries out its business activities in India. If a non-resident company has a PE in India, it is subject to taxation on the income attributable to that PE.

Furthermore, the Indian government has also signed various tax treaties with other countries to avoid double taxation and ensure that income generated from digital activities is not taxed twice. It is important to note that the taxation of the digital economy is a complex and evolving area, and governments around the world are continuously exploring new ways to effectively tax digital activities.

Therefore, it is advisable for businesses operating in the digital economy to stay updated with the latest tax laws and regulations to ensure compliance.

Chapter 9:
Land and Property Law Loopholes

Land and property laws in India are governed by various legislations, including the Transfer of Property Act, 1882, the Registration Act, 1908, and the Indian Contract Act, 1872, among others. While these laws aim to provide a comprehensive framework for the transfer and ownership of land and property, there may be certain loopholes or areas of ambiguity that can be exploited.

Some potential loopholes in land and property laws in India include:

1. Benami Transactions: Benami transactions refer to transactions where a property is held by one person but the consideration for the property is provided by another person. This practice is illegal under the Benami Transactions (Prohibition) Act, 1988. However, there may be instances where individuals use benami transactions to evade taxes or hide their ownership of properties.

2. Land Ceiling Laws: Land ceiling laws aim to prevent the concentration of land in the hands of a few individuals. However, there have been instances where individuals have found loopholes in these laws by transferring land to family members or creating multiple entities to hold land, thereby circumventing the land ceiling limits.

3. Illegal Conversions: In some cases, individuals may illegally convert agricultural land into non-agricultural land

for commercial or residential purposes. This can be done by bribing officials or through fraudulent means, thereby bypassing the restrictions on land use.

4. Encroachments: Encroachments refer to unauthorized occupation of land or property. Despite laws and regulations in place to prevent encroachments, there are instances where individuals or groups illegally occupy land and establish structures, often with the intention of regularizing their occupation through political or legal means.

5. Inadequate Title Verification: Due diligence in verifying the title of a property is crucial to ensure a legal and valid transfer. However, there have been cases where individuals have purchased properties without conducting proper title verification, leading to disputes and legal complications later on.

It is important to note that exploiting these loopholes is illegal and can result in legal consequences. The government and relevant authorities are continuously working to address these issues and strengthen land and property laws to prevent such loopholes from being exploited.

9.1 Land Acquisition and Rehabilitation

Land Acquisition and Rehabilitation refers to the process by which the government acquires land from private individuals or organizations for public purposes, such as infrastructure development, industrial projects, urbanization, or social welfare programs.

In India, land acquisition is governed by the Land Acquisition Act, 1894, which was recently replaced by the Right to Fair Compensation and Transparency in Land Acquisition, Rehabilitation and Resettlement Act, 2013 (LARR Act).

Under the LARR Act, the government can acquire land for public purposes, but it must follow a transparent and fair process. The Act provides for the payment of compensation to landowners, as well as rehabilitation and resettlement of affected families. The compensation must be based on the market value of the land, and additional benefits such as annuity, employment, and housing may also be provided.

The Act also lays down certain procedures that must be followed during the land acquisition process. These include conducting a social impact assessment to determine the potential adverse effects on affected families and communities, obtaining the consent of at least 70% of affected families for acquiring land for public-private partnership projects, and conducting a public hearing to address any grievances or objections.

The Act also emphasizes the importance of rehabilitation and resettlement of affected families. It mandates the preparation of a Rehabilitation and Resettlement Plan, which must include provisions for alternative livelihoods, housing, and basic amenities for the affected families. The Act also provides for the establishment of a Rehabilitation and Resettlement Authority at the state and national levels to oversee the implementation of these provisions. However, the implementation of the LARR Act has faced challenges and criticism. Some argue that the Act is still not comprehensive enough to protect the rights of affected families and ensure their proper rehabilitation. There have been concerns about the lack of transparency and accountability in the land acquisition process, as well as the displacement and loss of livelihoods faced by affected communities.

Overall, land acquisition and rehabilitation in India is a complex and contentious issue, with the need to balance the development needs of the country with the protection of the rights and welfare of affected individuals and communities.

9.2 Encroachment and Illegal Constructions

Encroachment and illegal constructions are serious issues in India, as they violate various laws and regulations. Encroachment refers to the unauthorized occupation or use of someone else's property, whether it is public or private land.

Illegal constructions, on the other hand, refer to any building or structure that is constructed without obtaining the necessary permissions and approvals from the relevant authorities. In India, encroachment and illegal constructions are governed by various laws and regulations at the national, state, and local levels. The most important legislation in this regard is the Indian Penal Code (IPC), which criminalizes encroachment and illegal constructions. Under the IPC, encroachment is considered a criminal offense and can attract penalties such as fines and imprisonment. Additionally, there are specific laws and regulations that deal with encroachment and illegal constructions in different states and cities.

For example, in Delhi, the Delhi Development Authority (DDA) Act and the Master Plan for Delhi regulate land use and construction activities. Any unauthorized construction in violation of these laws can be demolished by the authorities. To address the issue of encroachment and illegal constructions, the government and local authorities regularly carry out drives to identify and demolish such structures. They also encourage citizens to report any instances of encroachment or illegal constructions to the relevant authorities.

It is important for individuals and developers to obtain the necessary permissions and approvals before undertaking any construction activities to avoid legal consequences. Authorities are also taking steps to streamline the approval process and make it more transparent to discourage illegal constructions.

Overall, encroachment and illegal constructions are serious offenses in India, and the government is taking measures to curb these activities and enforce the law.

9.3 Title Disputes and Fraudulent Transfers

Title disputes and fraudulent transfers are two separate legal issues that can arise in the context of property ownership and transactions. Title disputes refer to conflicts or disagreements over the rightful ownership or possession of a property. These disputes can arise due to various reasons, such as conflicting claims of ownership, unclear or defective title documents, boundary disputes, or illegal transfers of property. Resolving title disputes typically involves legal proceedings, such as filing a lawsuit in a civil court, presenting evidence of ownership, and seeking a court order to establish or confirm the rightful owner of the property.

On the other hand, fraudulent transfers involve the illegal or improper transfer of property with the intention to deceive or defraud others. This can include transferring property to avoid creditors, hiding assets during bankruptcy proceedings, or transferring property to a third party to avoid legal obligations or liabilities. Fraudulent transfers are generally considered void or unenforceable under the law, and the affected parties may seek legal remedies to undo the transfer and recover their rights or assets. In India, title disputes and fraudulent transfers are governed by various laws, including the Transfer of Property Act, 1882, the Indian Contract Act, 1872, and the Indian Registration Act, 1908. Additionally, specific laws and regulations may apply depending on the nature of the property involved, such as the Real Estate (Regulation and Development) Act, 2016 for real estate transactions.

It is important for individuals and businesses to ensure that they have clear and valid title documents for their properties, and to be cautious of any suspicious or fraudulent transfers. In case of any disputes or concerns, seeking legal advice from a qualified lawyer is advisable to understand the applicable laws and take appropriate legal action.

9.4 Rent Control and Tenancy Laws

Rent control and tenancy laws in India are governed by various acts and regulations at both the central and state levels. These laws aim to protect the rights of tenants and regulate the relationship between landlords and tenants. The main legislation governing rent control and tenancy laws in India is the Rent Control Act, which varies from state to state.

Some of the key provisions of these acts include:

1. Rent Control: The acts regulate the maximum rent that can be charged by landlords for residential and commercial properties. The rent is usually determined based on factors such as the location, size, and amenities of the property.

2. Security Deposit: Landlords are allowed to collect a security deposit from tenants, which is usually a certain number of months' rent. The acts specify the maximum amount that can be collected as a security deposit and the conditions for its refund.

3. Tenancy Agreements: The acts require landlords and tenants to enter into a written agreement, commonly known as a lease or rent agreement. This agreement outlines the terms and conditions of the tenancy, including the rent amount, duration, and other rights and obligations of both parties.

4. Eviction: The acts provide guidelines for eviction of tenants by landlords. Landlords can evict tenants on specific grounds, such as non-payment of rent, subletting without permission, or misuse of the property. However, the acts also provide protection to tenants against arbitrary eviction and specify the procedure to be followed for eviction.

5. Maintenance and Repairs: The acts impose certain responsibilities on landlords to maintain the rented property in a habitable condition. Landlords are required to carry out

necessary repairs and maintenance work and ensure that the property is fit for occupation.

It is important to note that the specific provisions of rent control and tenancy laws may vary from state to state in India. Therefore, it is advisable to refer to the relevant state-specific legislation for detailed information.

9.5 Real Estate Regulation and Development

The Real Estate Regulation and Development (RERA) Act is a law enacted by the Indian government in 2016 to regulate the real estate sector in the country. The main objective of the RERA Act is to protect the interests of homebuyers and promote transparency and accountability in the real estate industry.

Under the RERA Act, all real estate projects with an area of more than 500 square meters or more than eight apartments must be registered with the respective state's Real Estate Regulatory Authority (RERA). The registration process requires developers to provide detailed information about the project, including the timeline for completion, the layout plans, and the financial details. The RERA Act also mandates that developers deposit 70% of the funds received from homebuyers in a separate escrow account. This provision ensures that developers use the funds for the specific project and prevents diversion of funds to other projects.

The RERA Act also establishes a mechanism for resolving disputes between homebuyers and developers. It requires developers to provide a clear and transparent grievance redressal mechanism, and also provides for the establishment of Real Estate Appellate Tribunals to hear appeals against the decisions of the Regulatory Authority. The RERA Act also imposes penalties on developers for non-compliance with the provisions of the Act. These penalties can include imprisonment and fines.

Overall, the RERA Act aims to bring transparency, accountability, and efficiency in the real estate sector in India, and provide a level playing field for both developers and homebuyers. It seeks to protect the interests of homebuyers and ensure timely completion of projects.

Chapter 10: Reforms and Solutions

There are several reforms and solutions that have been proposed or implemented in Indian laws to address various issues and challenges. Some of these include:

1. Criminal Justice Reforms: The Indian government has introduced several reforms to improve the criminal justice system, such as the introduction of fast-track courts to expedite the trial process, the use of technology for better case management, and the establishment of specialized courts for specific offenses like sexual offenses against women.

2. Women's Rights and Safety: In recent years, there have been significant efforts to strengthen laws related to women's rights and safety. The Criminal Law (Amendment) Act, 2013, commonly known as the Nirbhaya Act, was enacted to provide stricter punishment for sexual offenses against women. Additionally, the government has launched initiatives like the Beti Bachao Beti Padhao (Save the Girl Child, Educate the Girl Child) campaign to promote gender equality and empower women.

3. Legal Aid and Access to Justice: The government has taken steps to improve access to justice for marginalized sections of society by expanding the legal aid system. The Legal Services Authorities Act, 1987, provides free legal aid to the poor and marginalized sections of society.

Additionally, initiatives like the e-Courts project aim to digitize court processes and make them more accessible to the public.

4. Corporate Governance Reforms: In order to promote transparency and accountability in corporate practices, the government has introduced reforms in corporate governance laws. The Companies Act, 2013, introduced several provisions to enhance corporate governance standards, such as the establishment of independent directors, mandatory rotation of auditors, and increased disclosure requirements.

5. Intellectual Property Rights (IPR) Reforms: The Indian government has taken steps to strengthen the intellectual property rights regime in the country. The introduction of the National Intellectual Property Rights Policy in 2016 aimed to promote innovation and creativity by providing a robust legal framework for the protection of intellectual property rights.

6. Environmental Protection: The government has implemented various laws and regulations to protect the environment and promote sustainable development. The Environment (Protection) Act, 1986, provides the legal framework for environmental protection and conservation. Additionally, the government has launched initiatives like the Swachh Bharat Abhiyan (Clean India Mission) to address issues of sanitation and waste management.

These are just a few examples of the reforms and solutions that have been implemented or proposed in Indian laws. The government continues to work towards addressing various challenges and improving the legal framework to ensure justice, equality, and development in the country.

10.1 Judicial Reforms and Case Management

Judicial reforms and case management are crucial aspects of the Indian legal system. These reforms aim to improve the efficiency, transparency, and accessibility of the judiciary, ensuring timely justice delivery to the citizens. Here are some key aspects of judicial reforms and case management in India:

1. Case Management: Case management involves the effective and efficient handling of cases by the judiciary. It includes various measures such as setting timelines for different stages of the case, monitoring case progress, and ensuring timely disposal of cases. Case management techniques like alternative dispute resolution (ADR) methods, including mediation and arbitration, are also encouraged to reduce the burden on the courts.

2. E-Courts: The Indian judiciary has been actively implementing e-courts to digitize court processes and reduce paperwork. E-filing, e-summons, and e-payment facilities are being introduced to streamline case management and make it more accessible to litigants. The National Judicial Data Grid (NJDG) provides real-time information on case status, enabling litigants to track their cases online.

3. Fast Track Courts: To address the issue of pending cases and reduce the backlog, fast track courts have been established. These courts focus on expediting the trial of specific types of cases, such as those related to sexual

offenses, child abuse, and economic offenses. Fast track courts aim to ensure speedy justice and deterrence.

4. Alternative Dispute Resolution (ADR): ADR mechanisms like mediation, arbitration, and conciliation are being promoted as an alternative to traditional litigation. These methods help parties resolve disputes outside the court system, saving time and costs. The government has enacted laws like the Arbitration and Conciliation Act, 1996, to encourage the use of ADR methods.

5. Judicial Reforms: Various judicial reforms have been initiated to improve the functioning of the judiciary. These include the appointment of more judges to reduce the burden on existing courts, enhancing infrastructure facilities, and providing training to judges and court staff. The National Judicial Appointments Commission (NJAC) Act, 2014, aimed to reform the process of judicial appointments but was struck down by the Supreme Court in 2015.

6. Legal Aid and Access to Justice: The Indian legal system recognizes the importance of providing legal aid to the marginalized and underprivileged sections of society. The Legal Services Authorities Act, 1987, establishes legal aid committees to ensure access to justice for all. Legal aid clinics and Lok Adalats (people's courts) are set up to provide free legal assistance and resolve disputes amicably.

Overall, judicial reforms and case management in India are aimed at improving the efficiency and effectiveness of the legal system, reducing the backlog of cases, and ensuring timely justice delivery to all citizens. These reforms are essential for upholding the rule of law and protecting the rights of individuals.

10.2 Legislative Amendments and Policy Changes

Legislative amendments and policy changes refer to the modifications made to existing laws and regulations or the introduction of new policies by the government or legislative bodies. These changes are implemented to address emerging issues, improve governance, and ensure the laws are in line with the changing needs of society.

In India, legislative amendments and policy changes are carried out through a systematic process involving various stages. The process typically involves the following steps:

1. Identification of the need for change: The government or relevant authorities identify the need for legislative amendments or policy changes based on various factors such as societal changes, emerging challenges, or international obligations.

2. Proposal and drafting: Once the need for change is identified, the concerned ministry or department prepares a proposal for the amendment or policy change. This proposal is then drafted into a bill or policy document.

3. Consultation and stakeholder engagement: Before the bill or policy document is finalized, it is often shared with relevant stakeholders, including experts, industry representatives, civil society organizations, and the public. Their inputs and feedback are considered to ensure a comprehensive and inclusive approach.

4. Legislative process: In the case of legislative amendments, the bill is introduced in the Parliament or State Legislature, depending on the jurisdiction. It goes through multiple readings, debates, and voting before it is

passed as an amendment to the existing law. Policy changes, on the other hand, may not require legislative approval and can be implemented through executive orders or notifications.

5. Implementation and enforcement: Once the legislative amendments or policy changes are approved, they are implemented by the concerned authorities. This may involve creating new regulations, guidelines, or procedures to ensure effective enforcement.

6. Monitoring and evaluation: After the implementation, the impact of the legislative amendments or policy changes is monitored and evaluated to assess their effectiveness. If necessary, further modifications or adjustments may be made based on the evaluation findings.

It is important to note that legislative amendments and policy changes can cover a wide range of areas, including social welfare, economic reforms, environmental protection, criminal justice, labor laws, healthcare, education, and many others. The process and requirements for making changes may vary depending on the specific area and the level of government involved (central or state).

10.3 Strengthening Law Enforcement and Investigation

Strengthening law enforcement and investigation is crucial for maintaining law and order in any country, including India. It involves improving the capabilities and resources of law enforcement agencies to effectively prevent and combat crime, as well as ensuring a fair and efficient investigation process.

In India, several measures have been taken to strengthen law enforcement and investigation. These include:

1. Modernization of Police Forces: The government has initiated various schemes and programs to modernize the police forces across the country. This includes providing better infrastructure, equipment, and training to the police personnel.

2. Capacity Building: Efforts are being made to enhance the skills and capabilities of law enforcement officers through specialized training programs. This includes training in areas such as forensic science, cybercrime investigation, and counter-terrorism.

3. Use of Technology: The adoption of technology has played a significant role in strengthening law enforcement and investigation. This includes the use of CCTV cameras for surveillance, biometric identification systems, and digitization of records to improve efficiency and transparency.

4. Strengthening Forensic Capabilities: The establishment of forensic laboratories and the enhancement of their capabilities have been prioritized. This helps in the scientific investigation of crimes and ensures the collection and preservation of evidence.

5. Collaboration and Coordination: Effective coordination and collaboration between different law enforcement agencies, such as the police, intelligence agencies, and judiciary, are essential for successful investigation and prosecution of crimes. Specialized units like the National Investigation Agency (NIA) have been established to handle specific types of crimes.

6. Legal Reforms: Regular review and amendment of laws are undertaken to ensure they are in line with the changing nature of crimes. This includes enacting new legislation to address emerging challenges, such as cybercrime and terrorism.

7. Community Engagement: Building trust and cooperation between law enforcement agencies and the community is crucial for effective crime prevention and investigation. Community policing initiatives are being implemented to encourage citizen participation and support.

8. Strengthening Prosecution: Along with law enforcement, the prosecution process also needs to be strengthened. This includes providing adequate resources and training to public prosecutors, establishing fast-track courts for speedy trials, and ensuring witness protection. Overall, strengthening law enforcement and investigation in India requires a multi-faceted approach that includes modernization, capacity building, technology adoption, legal reforms, and community engagement. These efforts aim to ensure a safe and secure environment for all citizens and uphold the rule of law.

10.4 Public Awareness and Legal Education

Public awareness and legal education are crucial aspects of any society. They play a significant role in promoting a just and fair legal system and ensuring that individuals are aware of their rights and responsibilities under the law.

In India, several initiatives have been taken to enhance public awareness and legal education. One of the key initiatives is the National Legal Services Authority

(NALSA), which was established under the Legal Services Authorities Act, 1987. NALSA aims to provide free legal aid and services to the marginalized and underprivileged sections of society. It also conducts legal literacy programs to educate people about their rights and the legal processes.

The government, along with various non-governmental organizations (NGOs), has also launched several campaigns and programs to raise public awareness about specific legal issues. For example, campaigns have been conducted to educate people about the importance of voting, the rights of women and children, and the prevention of domestic violence.

Legal education is another important aspect of public awareness. The Bar Council of India, which regulates legal education in the country, has made it mandatory for law schools to include legal aid clinics in their curriculum. These clinics provide practical training to law students and also offer free legal services to the needy.

Furthermore, the government has introduced legal literacy programs in schools and colleges to educate students about their rights and responsibilities. These programs aim to create a legal awareness among the younger generation and empower them to become responsible citizens. In recent years, the use of technology has also played a significant role in enhancing public awareness and legal education.

Online platforms and mobile applications have been developed to provide easy access to legal information and resources. These platforms offer legal advice, information about legal procedures, and access to legal documents. Despite these efforts, there is still a need for continuous improvement in public awareness and legal education in India. The legal system can be complex and intimidating for many individuals, especially those from marginalized communities. Therefore, it is essential to ensure that legal information and resources are easily accessible and understandable to all sections of society.

10.5 International Cooperation and Comparative Studies

International cooperation and comparative studies are important aspects of the field of law. They involve the study and analysis of legal systems and practices in different countries, as well as the collaboration and exchange of information and resources between nations. International cooperation in law refers to the efforts made by countries to work together on legal issues of mutual interest. This can include sharing information and best practices, coordinating efforts to combat transnational crimes, and establishing treaties and agreements to promote cooperation in areas such as trade, human rights, and environmental protection.

Comparative studies in law involve the examination and comparison of different legal systems and their approaches to various legal issues. This can help identify similarities and differences between legal systems, highlight best practices, and inform the development and reform of laws in different countries. In the context of Indian laws, international cooperation and comparative studies play a crucial role. India is a member of various international organizations and has entered into numerous bilateral and multilateral agreements with other countries. These agreements cover a wide range of areas, including trade, investment, extradition, and mutual legal assistance.

Through international cooperation, India can collaborate with other countries to address common legal challenges, such as terrorism, money laundering, and cybercrime. It can also benefit from the exchange of information and expertise, which can help improve its legal system and practices. Comparative studies of Indian laws with those of other countries can provide valuable insights into areas where reforms may be needed. By studying the legal systems of other countries, India can identify best practices and innovative approaches that can be adopted to enhance its own legal framework. Overall, international cooperation and comparative studies are essential for the development and improvement of Indian laws. They enable India to engage with the global community, learn from the experiences of other countries, and contribute to the advancement of international legal norms and standards.

www.ingramcontent.com/pod-product-compliance
Lightning Source LLC
LaVergne TN
LVHW072336080526
838199LV00109B/438